D1566692

The Civil Rights Injunction

THE
CIVIL RIGHTS
INJUNCTION.

Owen M. Fiss

Indiana University Press   Bloomington & London

Manufactured in the United States of America

Library of Congress Cataloging in Publication Data
Fiss, Owen M.
    The civil rights injunction.
    Includes bibliographical references and index.
    1. Injunction—United States.   2. Civil rights—
United States.   I. Title.
KF9014.F5   342'.73'0850269   78-2052
ISBN 0-253-31356-2   1 2 3 4 5 82 81 80 79 78

Foreword

This book is based on the Addison C. Harris Lectures delivered by Professor Owen M. Fiss of the Yale Law School at the Indiana University–Bloomington School of Law on April 5 and 6, 1976. The Harris lectureship, endowed by India Harris and named for her husband, an eminent Indiana lawyer and public servant, was established, in the language of her will, "for the purpose of instructing lawyers and students of the law in the higher and more advanced questions and theories thereof by obtaining the assistance and services of men of great ability and renown to give practical lectures upon such subjects of the law as a science or system of jurisprudence."

From 1949, when the first lecture was given, the list of these lecturers of "great ability and renown" includes, in addition to Professor Fiss, Robert H. Bork, Professor of Law, Yale Law School; Guido Calabresi, Professor of Law, Yale Law School; Morton J. Horwitz, Professor of Law, Harvard University School of Law; Charles J. Meyers, Dean and Professor of Law, Stanford School of Law; Frank I. Michelman, Professor of Law, Harvard University School of Law; S. F. C. Milsom, then Professor of Legal History in the London School of Economics; Charles R. Nesson, Professor of Law, Harvard University School of Law; and Monrad G. Paulsen, Dean and Professor of Law, University of Virginia School of Law.

India Harris was thoughtful enough to direct in her will that the lectures be published and thereby made available to a wider audience. Through the cooperation of the Indiana University Press, the School of Law is happy to comply with this direction by publishing Professor Fiss's valuable study of the civil rights injunction.

He brings to this work a distinguished scholarly career and also an active involvement with civil rights litigation since the sixties, when he held a succession of positions as Law Clerk to Thurgood Marshall, then a Circuit Judge; Law Clerk to Supreme Court Justice William J. Brennan; and Special Assistant to John Doar, then Assistant Attorney General in charge of the Civil Rights Division, Department of Justice. Convinced that the traditional attitudes toward the injunction are no longer valid in light of the civil rights experience, Professor Fiss now presents us with the first thorough reevaluation of this controversial remedy since Frankfurter and Greene's *The Labor Injunction*, written in the twenties.

Sheldon J. Plager, *Dean*
School of Law
Indiana University

Contents

The Civil Rights Injunction

I

The Triumph of <u>Brown</u>

Traditionally the relationship among remedies has been hierarchical. Remedies are ranked. Those near the top are the ones preferred. Those near the bottom may be utilized, but only if certain special conditions are met—conditions that are not placed on the other remedies.

This notion of a hierarchy of remedies has been one of the hallmarks of our legal system. Even more striking is the fact that in this hierarchy the injunction has classically been assigned a subordinate position. The injunction has been deemed an "extraordinary" remedy, to be used only if all else fails. The injunction should not issue, so tradition tells us, until it can be demonstrated that other remedies are inadequate. These doctrines are the inheritance of an age when the injunction was paradigmatically used to protect property rights, such as those associated with the ownership of land.

In the late nineteenth century a new paradigm emerged—the labor injunction. The injunction then came to be used as a tool of industrial warfare, as a means of preventing the organization of labor and breaking strikes. This usage was best symbolized by the celebrated *Debs* case,[1] involving an injunction against Eugene Debs and his followers in the American Railway Union. They struck in support of the Pullman workers and managed to tie up the railways of the nation. The Supreme Court built on the law of nuisance, more particularly, that branch of the law of nuisance authorizing injunctions to remove physical obstruction to public highways and navigable waterways, and sustained the injunction—nominally not to deny the right to strike, but only to remove the obstruction to interstate commerce.

The strike occurred in 1894 and the Court sustained the injunction a year later, in the context of reviewing Debs's contempt conviction. Long before the Supreme Court spoke, the injunction had its bite—federal troops had been deployed, Eugene Debs was arrested and removed from the field, the strike was broken, and the American Railway Union destroyed. What the Supreme Court added, however, was legitimacy—it gave a legitimacy to the practices represented by the *Debs* injunction. The Court showed that only lip service need be paid to the traditional restraints on the issuance of injunctions, and in this lesson it altered the traditional conception of the injunction and its place in the remedial hierarchy. The Court promised that in matters of industrial warfare the injunction could be the remedy of first recourse, and in the next decade or two that promise was fulfilled.

At roughly the same time, during the ascendancy of the labor injunction, the injunction also became an important instrument for fighting Progressivism—conceived in this instance as a program to reform and regulate business practices. The Progressives attained a number of legislative successes, including laws to regulate the rates of railroads and to impose maximum hours of employment, and the various business interests that lost the legislative battles often took their grievance to the courts.

Usually their claim was tendered by way of a defense in a criminal prosecution. The Supreme Court sustained such a claim in *Lochner* v. *New York*,[2] invalidating a state law prohibiting employees from working in bakeries more than sixty hours a week. *Lochner* was decided in 1905, and in 1908, in the midst of the public outcry over that decision, the Supreme

Court sustained a similar anti-Progressivism claim, this time cast in the injunctive form. In *Ex parte Young*,[3] in an opinion written by Justice Peckham, also the author of *Lochner*, the Supreme Court allowed a federal injunction to be used against the Attorney General of Minnesota, to prevent him from enforcing a state law proscribing maximum rates for railroads. *Ex parte Young* was viewed as an integral part of the judicial assault on Progressivism, and the reaction to it was aggravated by the specter of a federal judge holding the attorney general of a state in contempt, particularly when the contemptuous act consisted of nothing more than the commencement of a law suit in state court, as a means of enforcing the maximum rate law. The salience of the injunction was thereby heightened and the coalition of those wary of the labor injunction broadened. The dissatisfaction with the labor injunction was generalized to all injunctions.

This dissatisfaction received congressional expression. Some of the restrictions that resulted were procedural—for example, the 1910 Act requiring a three-judge court for the issuance of interlocutory injunctions against state statutes[4] and the 1914 Clayton Act confining temporary restraining orders to situations of true necessity, narrowing the binding effect of injunctions to parties, and guaranteeing trial by jury in certain contempt proceedings.[5] Other restrictions were substantive— the Clayton Act sought to protect the rights to strike and picket, and the right peacefully to persuade others to engage in this activity, by prohibiting federal court injunctions against such conduct;[6] the 1932 Norris-LaGuardia Act went one step further and altogether denied the federal courts the power to issue injunctions in labor disputes.[7] Many of these federal enactments had state counterparts.

Expressions of dissatisfaction also arose in the academic culture. Felix Frankfurter and a graduate student of his, Nathan Greene, writing in the late 1920s after the first wave

of congressional intervention and on the eve of the Norris–
LaGuardia Act, gave us their now classic book *The Labor Injunction*. Frankfurter and Greene built their case out of the
abuses of the injunction as a tool of industrial warfare; the
book was a brief for the soon-to-be enacted Norris–LaGuardia
Act. But we—the post–World War II, post–New Deal genera-
tion—received their book as a *general* statement about the
injunction, divorced from the particular substantive claims it
served. Their book, like the congressional intervention, was
viewed—or even more, cited—as an argument to return the
injunction to its traditional position as a modest and narrowly
circumscribed remedy.

In the 1950s the traditional conceptions derived from the
property injunction were once again called into question. This
time the revision was wrought not by the labor injunction or
the anti-Progressivism injunction, but by a new paradigm—
the civil rights injunction. *In re Debs* and *Ex parte Young,* the
legalistic symbols of previous revolutions, were supplanted by
Brown v. *Board of Education*.[8]

Brown gave the injunction a special prominence. School
desegregation became one of the prime litigative chores of the
courts in the period 1954–74, and in these cases the typical
remedy was the injunction. School desegregation not only gave
the injunction a greater currency, it also presented the injunction with new challenges, in terms of both the enormity and
the kinds of tasks it was assigned. The injunction was to be
used to restructure educational systems throughout the nation.

The impact of *Brown* on our remedial jurisprudence—giving
a primacy to the injunction—was not confined to school desegregation. It also extended to civil rights cases in general, and
beyond civil rights to litigation involving electoral reappor-
tionment, mental hospitals, prisons, trade practices, and the
environment. Having desegregated the schools of Alabama, it
was only natural for Judge Johnson to try to reform the mental

hospitals and then the prisons of the state in the name of human rights—the right to treatment or to be free from cruel and unusual punishment—and to attempt this Herculean feat through the injunction.[9] And he was not alone. The same logic was manifest in the action of other judges, North and South.

These developments rested in part on certain normative premises, especially ones concerning the legitimacy of *Brown* and the exercise of the injunctive power implied in that case. At the outset, *Brown* met with a hostile reception, but over time it was generally viewed as legitimate. Indeed, by the late 1960s, *Brown* was viewed as so legitimate that it commonly functioned as an *axiom*—a decision of unquestioned correctness, a starting point for normative reasoning in domains far removed from schools and race. It was the foundation for arguments of the form, "If this use of the injunction is denied, *Brown* is being denied, and *therefore,* this use cannot be denied."[10]

Today the axiomatic status of *Brown* is in the balance. The Second Reconstruction is not being dismantled, at least not yet, but it has been brought to a halt. The momentum has been lost. The formal validity of *Brown* is not denied; it is, however, only conceded. It is not embraced, nor endorsed. For a controlling bloc on the present Supreme Court, *Brown* is not a starting point, but rather an exception, to be tolerated rather than built on. Congress has turned from civil rights laws to antibusing enactments. Similar trends are gaining momentum in academic circles, as witnessed by the surprising attention given to Lino Graglia's book *Disaster by Decree* (1976), and Raoul Berger's book *Government by Judiciary* (1977)—touchingly the title of another book, one by Louis Boudin, written some forty years ago in reaction to *Debs, Ex parte Young,* and their progeny. From all signs we now seem to be in a period of reconstitution.

In this period the injunction has once again become a very special target of attack. Reactionary forces have been attentive to the remedy. Seeking to return the injunction to a subordinate place in the remedial hierarchy, they have entered a plea on behalf of traditional doctrine that would curtail its use. My purpose is to show that this doctrine is without adequate theoretical foundation. There is no reason why the injunction should be disfavored as a remedy, why it should be subject to restrictions not applied to other remedies. I will urge that the traditional view give way to a nonhierarchical conception of remedies, where there is no presumptive remedy, but rather a context-specific evaluation of the advantages and disadvantages of each form of relief. It should not be necessary to establish the inadequacy of alternative remedies before the injunction becomes available; at the same time, the superiority of the injunction should not be presumed, but rather dependent on an analysis of its technical advantages and the system of power allocation that it implies.

My plea is not confined to the civil rights injunction, but should extend to all types of injunctions. I speak of the triumph of *Brown* and the civil rights injunction because the shift of paradigms has been intellectually liberating. First, it has uncovered a rich body of experience that can be drawn on for defining the injunction and understanding its relationship to other remedies. Second, it has enabled me to abstract right from remedy. I now see that the argument presented by the traditionalists, such as Frankfurter and Greene, against the injunction was neither general nor dispassionate; rather, it preyed on our substantive sensibilities—our belief that the claim being served by the labor injunction—to suppress the organization of labor—was unjust. The civil rights injunction, on the other hand, permits us to look at the injunction through a different substantive lens—a belief that the underlying claim—to achieve equality for the racial minority—is just. It invites us to imagine that the substantive claim *could* be just, and to ask then whether the classical position of the injunction in the remedial hierarchy—one of subordination—can be justified.

II

The Sources of Uniqueness

We must begin with the definition of the injunction. So much of the argument for the traditional remedial hierarchy depends on a mistaken conception of the injunction, either on exaggerated notions of its uniqueness or on an incorrect identification of the elements that make it unique.

The law has long embraced a pluralism with regard to injunctions, accepting the idea that there are categories or species of injunctions. But for the most part the pluralism has been too limited—content to distinguish interlocutory and final injunctions, or perhaps mandatory or prohibitory ones. I would like to expand the pluralism and introduce three new categories: the preventive injunction, which seeks to prohibit some discrete act or series of acts from occurring in the future; the reparative injunction, which compels the defendant to engage in a course of action that seeks to correct the effects of a past wrong; and the structural injunction, which seeks to effectuate the reorganization of an ongoing social institution. The preventive injunction coincided with the paradigms of an earlier age, the property, labor, and anti-Progressivism injunctions. It was the civil rights experience that brought both the reparative and structural categories into focus, giving them a special prominence and legitimacy.

Equipped with these new categories, I think we will be in a better position to assess the alleged uniqueness of the injunction. Classic doctrine, such as the irreparable injury requirement, has been primarily addressed to the preventive injunction, and paradoxically, that injunction bears a striking resemblance to other remedies. The preventive injunction might be viewed as a mini-criminal statute, though more individuated, more decentralized, and with greater power invested in the judge. With the newer categories, those with roots in civil rights litigation, we seem to move in two different directions. The reparative injunction closely resembles the damage judgment and might be viewed as an in-kind damage award, while the structural injunction emerges, so I will maintain, as a truly unique legal instrument.

A. THE CONTENT OF THE INJUNCTION

1. Prevention

Justice Story described the unique office of the injunction as preventive justice:[1] the injunction is an instrument designed to prevent a wrong from occurring in the future. There are two important senses in which this proposition is false: it overstates the claim of uniqueness and takes insufficient account of reparative and structural injunctions.

In asserting the supposed uniqueness of the injunction, Story is comparing it to the damage award or criminal conviction; these remedies have an effect upon the future conduct of both the individual against whom a judgment is entered (specific deterrence) and society in general (general deterrence). Yet they are retrospective remedies, because a necessary condition for each (putting aside the category of inchoate crimes) is that a wrong has occurred. This is not true for the classic injunction, the preventive one.

Story's claim of uniqueness, however, involves a false comparison. The preventive injunction should not be compared to the damage award or the criminal conviction, but rather to the rules of conduct underlying those judicial judgments—the liability rule or the criminal prohibition. Both the liability rule and the criminal prohibition are addressed to the future, and neither requires a past wrong in order to become operative. Each controls conduct through deterrence—the liability rule is backed by a threat to impose costs, and the criminal prohibition by a threat to punish. The preventive injunction operates in a similar fashion.

This can be seen more clearly if the injunctive process is divided into two phases: the issuance phase, in which the tribunal promulgates the rule of conduct, and the enforcement phase, in which sanctions are imposed for noncompliance with the previously promulgated rule of conduct. The enforcement phase can properly be compared to the damage action or criminal prosecution; all are retrospective in the sense that they are responsive to an antecedent wrong—a violation of a rule of conduct. The issuance phase of the injunctive process, on the other hand, should be compared with the promulgation of a rule of liability or a criminal prohibition: a past wrong is not a necessary condition for either, and the concern of each is to establish standards of future conduct.

The standard account also misleads in suggesting that prevention is the only concern of the injunction. Prevention may have been the exclusive office of the property, labor, and anti-Progressivism injunctions, but not of the civil rights injunction. Many civil rights injunctions are preventive: they decree that the defendant not discriminate in the future. But there are at least two species, two important species, that are more backward-looking.

The first is the structural injunction—the injunction seeking to effectuate the reform of a social institution. The most notable example is a decree seeking to bring about the reorganization of a school system from a "dual system" to a "unitary nonracial school system." Antecedents of these decrees might be found in the railroad reorganizations at the turn of the century[2] or, more recently, in the antitrust divestiture cases.[3] But it was school desegregation, I maintain, that gave these types of injunctions their contemporary saliency and legitimacy; in the wake of this experience, courts have attempted the structural reorganization of other institutions, such as hospitals and prisons, not just to vindicate a claim of racial equality, but also to vindicate other claims, such as the right against cruel and unusual punishment or the right to treatment.[4]

The other backward-looking injunction is the reparative injunction—an injunction that seeks to eliminate the effects of a past wrong, in this instance conceived as some discrete act or course of conduct. To see how it works, let us assume that a wrong has occurred (such as an act of discrimination). Then the mission of an injunction—classically conceived as a preventive instrument—would be to prevent the recurrence of the wrongful conduct in the future (stop discriminating and do not discriminate again). But in *United States* v. *Louisiana*,[5] a voting discrimination case, Justice Black identified still another mission for the injunction—the elimination of the *effects* of the past wrong (the past discrimination). The reparative injunction—long thought by the nineteenth-century textbook writers, such as High,[6] to be an analytical impossibility—was thereby legitimated. And in the same vein, election officials have been ordered not only to stop discriminating in future elections, but also to set aside a past election and to run a new election as a means of removing the taint of discrimination that infected the first one.[7] Similarly, public housing officials have been ordered both to cease discriminating on the basis of race in their future choices of sites and to build units in the white areas as a means of eliminating the effects of the past segregative policy (placing public housing projects only in the black areas of the city).[8]

The mission of these backward-looking injunctions—both the structural and the reparative variety—might be described so as to reduce the tension with the classical conception of the injunction as an exclusively preventive instrument. For the structural injunction it might be said that the purpose of reorganizing an institution is to prevent a wrong from recurring. And for the reparative injunction it might be said that being subjected to the continuing effects of a past wrong is itself an independent wrong, a wrong that is to occur in the future, and that the purpose of the injunction is to prevent *that* wrong. Without wholly denying the analytic integrity of these attempted reconceptualizations, let me suggest that both strain and obscure the underlying social realities.

The attempted reconceptualization of the structural injunction assumes that the wrong exists independently of the organizational structure, and that assumption is incorrect. The constitutional wrong is the structure itself; the reorganization is designed to bring the structure within constitutional bounds— not to minimize the chance of some other, discrete wrong occurring. Moreover, at least as a practical matter, a past wrong is required for the issuance of a structural injunction; the mere threat of a wrong in the future is not likely to be deemed sufficient to trigger the reform enterprise, even though such a threat is sufficient for the classic preventive injunction. A structural injunction is unlikely to issue without a judgment that the existing institutional arrangement is illegal, is now a wrong, and will continue to be wrongful unless corrected.

The attempt to make the reparative injunction appear preventive is similarly flawed. The redefinition fails to reflect the derivative nature of the future wrong—that the wrong supposedly to be prevented by the reparative injunction is analytically derived from a past wrong. A past wrong and its effects must be identified before we can even understand the future wrong to be prevented. The reconceptualization of the reparative injunction is no more persuasive than would be the claim that the damage award is preventive because it prevents the future wrong of leaving the victim uncompensated for his injuries. Both conceptions are highly contrived. And there is so little to be gained. It would be better to abandon this analytic scrimmage and simply accept one important lesson from the civil rights experience—that the office of the injunction need no longer be exclusively preventive.

2. Individuation

If I am correct in asserting that the preventive injunction is best compared to the liability rule or the criminal prohibition, in that all are preventive instruments, one striking difference readily comes to mind, namely, the individuated quality of the injunction. A liability rule or criminal prohibition, for example, makes it unlawful for landowners to use their property in a way that unreasonably interferes with the enjoyment of land by others. The injunction rests on or assumes these same generalized standards of conduct, but then introduces an individuated quality—it prohibits the defendant's cement factory from emitting smoke onto the plaintiff's land. The individuation of the injunction arises from the fact, first, that it is *addressed* to some clearly identified individual, not just the general citizenry; second, the *act* prohibited or required is described with a degree of specificity not found in a liability rule or criminal prohibition; and third, the *beneficiaries* of the decree are also more specifically delineated.[9]

Initially, we should observe the reach of this distinction. Individuation might serve to differentiate the typical preventive injunction from the liability rule or criminal prohibition, but it does not establish uniqueness for the reparative injunction. The true analog for that variety of injunction is the damage judgment, and the damage judgment seems as individuated as the reparative injunction. A more fundamental point to note is that individuation is but a *potential*. The injunction can be individuated, but it need not be; and to the extent that it is not, the resemblance increases between the injunction—particularly of the preventive variety—and other preventive instruments such as liability rules and criminal prohibitions. The property injunction might have been highly individuated as a rule; not so the civil rights injunction.

In terms of the decreed act, preventive injunctions have been characteristically broad. Almost all preventive injunctions in the civil rights area contain a provision that does little more than track the prohibition of the appropriate statute or constitutional command—do not discriminate on the basis of race. The broader the command the greater the threat to due process values, and the harder it is to impose severe sanctions—adequate notice of what constitutes a violation is likely to be lacking. On the other hand, broad commands make evasion more difficult and may deter even though severe sanctions are unlikely. Costs are imposed on the defendant by the very assertion of a claim of violation and the necessity of defending an enforcement proceeding.

With the other types of civil rights injunctions, the decreed act has been more individuated. The reparative injunction—promising to give in-kind compensation—has been specific in terms of the act prohibited or required. The very purpose of the injunction is to specify the compensation. With the structural injunction the story is more complicated: over time the decreed act becomes more and more specific, for example, detailing the dates on which choice forms are to be distributed, the ratio of blacks and whites in each school, the amount to be spent on books, etc. But this specificity emerges as a last resort. The original impulse in these structural cases was just the opposite—to use almost no specificity in describing the act required.

For the first decade, 1954–64, the typical school decree, to take the most common structural injunction, had two parts—one a broad prohibition (do not discriminate on the basis of race; do not maintain a "dual school system"), and the other a

requirement for the school board to submit a plan for transforming the "dual school system" into a "unitary, nonracial
school system." This plan-submission technique was an attempt
to have the defendants—as opposed to the plaintiffs or the
court—specify their own remedial steps. It reflected doctrinal
uncertainty (a lack of clarity as to what "unitary nonracial
school system" meant); strategic considerations (a desire to go
slowly or to be as uncoercive or unobtrusive as possible); and
a desire to capitalize on the expertise of the school board. The
technique of plan submission made eminent sense, and yet in
time courts saw the obvious—that these generalized decrees
would not effectively change the status quo. The same dynamics
that led to the violation in the first place would prevent the
defendant from using its knowledge and imagination against
itself, from tying its own hands too effectively or too stringently.
The school boards failed to plan for themselves. During the
second *Brown* decade, 1964–74, the courts began to write their
own plans and thus to be increasingly specific in describing the
steps for the structural reformation. The Supreme Court was
anxious to emphasize, however, that these "specifics" were to
be viewed as mere expedients—perhaps only of a temporary
duration—necessary to cope with the absence of good faith.[10]

The absence of individuation in the beneficiary component
of civil rights injunctions is even more striking, and does not
vary greatly among reparative, structural, and preventive injunctions. The beneficiary of the typical civil rights injunction
is not an individual, or even a collection of identifiable individuals; rather it is a social group—the blacks. The contours
of the benefitted group are determined not by the personal
characteristics of the person who happens to be the named
plaintiff, but rather by considerations of who should—as a
matter of fairness, efficacy, and equal protection theory—receive the benefit. This is not due to the procedural vessel, the
fact that the suits are formally brought as representative ac-

tions; it is due instead to the group character of the underlying substantive claim—the fact that racial discrimination impairs the status of an already disadvantaged group, blacks, and for that very reason is proscribed by the Equal Protection Clause.[11] Form follows substance.

The prominence of the class action in civil rights injunctive proceedings and the emergence in 1966 of a new type of class action—the b(2) action—were due to the group nature of the substantive claim.[12] Similarly the group nature of the substantive claim helps explain Executive participation in civil rights suits.[13] The superior litigative resources of the Executive might have provided the impetus, but it was the group nature of the substantive claim that facilitated that participation. The Executive was just as entitled to speak for the group as was the plaintiff or the civil rights organization standing behind the plaintiff —the self-appointed representatives of the group. And, of course, the beneficiaries of a decree issued in a suit brought by the United States are not in any sense individuated.

Developments in the addressee component paralleled the loss of individuation in the act and beneficiary components. Civil rights injunctions were typically addressed to the office, rather than the person. This was true even in cases where abuse of office was charged. Operationally this meant that in determining whether an injunction was needed, the misconduct of the predecessors in office would automatically be attributed to the incumbent; there was a tacking of misconduct. It also meant that, after issuance, the automatic substitution rule of Federal Rule of Civil Procedure 25(d) would be invoked. Rule 65(d) of the Federal Rules, which originated in the Clayton Act of 1914 as an attempt to confine the labor injunction, omits the word "successor" in the list of persons bound by a decree. Yet virtually no attention was given that omission in designing civil rights injunctions. The word "successor" was included in almost all civil rights injunctions, premised on the insight that the most important determination of official conduct is not the person but the office—defined not by the formal job description but by the traditions, culture, and surrounding political structures.[14]

This shift from person to office as addressee occurs along a vertical axis—over time. No one pays much attention to the person who happens to occupy the office at any particular time. It should also be noted that there has been a comparable development along the horizontal axis—at any one time large numbers of persons have been bound by the decree; injunctions have been made to "run against the world."

There was a need for a broad injunction in labor disputes. These disputes often involved mass conduct—countless picketers, strikers, and labor organizers—many of whom were not known to the employer. Often the labor injunction—including the *Debs* injunction—was addressed to anyone who happened to get actual notice of it. In the reaction to the labor injunction this scope was identified as an "abuse," a derogation of the principle enunciated by Lord Elden that only parties are bound.[15] This view obtained legislative approval in the Clayton Act of 1914 and was carried over to Federal Rule 65(d). It confined federal court injunctions to the parties (and their agents). By the 1930s, however, what appeared to be at stake was not just an English dictum or a congressional command, but, in the words of Justice Brandeis, "established principles of equity jurisdiction and procedure"[16]—a phrase that has the same resonance as a claim about the requirements of due process. Individuation was not just a practice, but rather an ideal.

The civil rights experience called this ideal into question. The substantive claim did not cause us to ignore procedural values, but rather to look at them with greater scrutiny. There was an urgent need for a legal instrument to deal, for example, with white political leaders and citizens' groups—not parties to the underlying school desegregation case—who were preventing black children from exercising rights under the decree, i.e., from attending formerly all white schools. This was manifest in one response to the Little Rock crisis—the enactment of 18 U.S.C. § 1509—making it a crime for *anyone* to interfere forcibly with the exercise of rights arising from a federal court decree.[17] The validity of the decree was not open to relitigation, and the individual who interfered with rights emanating from that decree was subject to criminal penalties. In that sense the nonparty was bound by the decree. A second departure from the ideal also had its roots in the Little Rock crisis, and in the crises surrounding the school closing in Alabama (1963) and the registration of James Meredith at Ole Miss (1962).[18] What emerged from these crises was an antiobstruction injunction— an injunction prohibiting interferences with the rights granted by another decree.

Initially these antiobstruction injunctions were granted against named individuals such as Governors Faubus, Barnett, and Wallace, and only after hearings, although the defendants in these antiobstruction proceedings were not allowed to question the correctness of the findings and conclusions of the underlying injunction. But starting in about 1966, in order to cope with the faceless mob, the antiobstruction decree took the form of an ex parte temporary restraining order against anyone with actual notice of the decree. Federal Rule 65(d) was brushed aside on the theory that it was only a codification of, rather than a limitation upon, the courts' common law powers. The underlying injunction (the one now being protected by the antiobstruction injunction) was described as having, "in effect, adjudicated the rights of the entire community with respect to the racial controversy surrounding the school system."[19] These words mark the distance we have come—because of the civil rights injunction—from the individuated ideal associated with the property injunction, and underscore the fact that even in the addressee component individuation is only a potential; to the extent that it is not realized, the comparison between the preventive injunction and its analogs is strengthened.

B. The Nature of the Injunctive Process

1. The Power of Initiation

Our legal system is characterized by two different models for formally allocating the power of initiating a judicial process: one allocates it to officers, the other to the citizenry. With the officer model, the power to initiate a lawsuit is centralized in the sense that it is vested in a limited number of governmental officials—the district attorney or Secretary of Labor. The citizen's role is a modest one. He may file a complaint with the government official, and, under the new jurisprudence disfavoring administrative discretion, he may even utilize procedures to make certain that the government official responds to the complaint in a nonarbitrary manner. But the power of initiation is in the government official. In contrast, the citizen model contemplates a wider dispersion of the power of initiation. The exercise of the power may be conditioned on certain requirements, some procedural (e.g., filing a complaint), some substantive (e.g., stating a claim for which relief can be given), and others financial (e.g., paying filing fees); and yet access is not formally blocked by some government officer who decides whether or not to proceed. The power to initiate litigation is vested in the citizen.

The injunctive process, like the damage process and unlike the criminal one, conforms to the decentralized citizen model. The power of initiation is allocated to the citizenry. This classification of injunctive proceedings needs no qualification if one focusses on the issuance phase and if the concern is with the property injunction. Qualifications must be introduced, however, if one's attention shifts to the enforcement phase and if sufficient account is taken of developments with the labor injunction, developments that are renewed by the civil rights injunction. Before turning to these qualifications, I should emphasize that even with them the predominant motif in the initiation sphere remains one of decentralization, comparable to the damage system.

Assume that a citizen initiates an injunctive suit, an injunction is issued, and the defendant does the act prohibited by the injunction. The citizen-plaintiff can commence an enforcement proceeding designed to coerce compliance with the injunction (the defendant is jailed until assurances are received that he will refrain from the prohibited act). He can also seek to obtain compensation for the harm caused by the violation. With these two varieties of contempt—the first is conditional-order civil contempt and the second is compensatory-damage civil contempt—the power of initiation is allocated to the citizen. There is a third type of contempt proceeding—criminal contempt; here the sanction is a finite jail sentence or fine, and the allocative scheme is more complicated. The power to initiate is shared by court and citizen.[20]

As a purely formal matter the power to initiate criminal contempt is allocated to the tribunal. It is important to recognize, however, that even on a formal level there is more decentralization in this allocative scheme than in that of the criminal system, where the power of initiation is vested in a district attorney or the Attorney General. For we are talking about an allocation to many trial judges. Each judge has considerable leeway. True, initiation in the criminal sphere may be delegated to an assistant district attorney, but in contrast to the assistant district attorney, each individual judge views himself as an autonomous actor. This view in part derives from the independence of the judge's commission and from the absence of the usual hierarchical controls by superiors (the appellate judges) over the incidents of the job, e.g., pay and promotion. It is reinforced by the knowledge that a decision *not* to proceed is generally unreviewable, and by the fact that even if it is reviewable, the standard of review is the lax abuse-of-discretion one.[21]

Moreover, as a practical matter, the citizen plays a large role in criminal contempt, perhaps even larger than the one he plays in the criminal system (as complaining witness). For the court, more than the district attorney, is conceived of as a passive institution. On occasion a judge can transcend that mind set and abandon his passive role. Yet, in order to do so, the judge has to overcome inertia, doctrines requiring him to act on the basis of general rules (often an inappropriate basis for making prosecutorial decisions), and the absence of proper staff for this function (e.g., investigators). Thus, for the most part, the tribunal depends heavily on the initiatives of the individual citizen for bringing the violation to light, and often for the presentation of the case. As a consequence, the practical allocation—though not the formal allocation—may be thought to be to the citizenry.

The relationship between the injunction and the decentralized citizen model for initiation is purely contingent, much like individuation. The officer model can be introduced even in the issuance phase. This is one of the important legacies of *Debs*.

In 1890 Congress passed the Sherman Antitrust Act; that law authorized the Attorney General to bring injunctive suits to prevent restraints of trade. *Debs* was in fact brought by the Attorney General under the Sherman Act, but the Supreme Court chose not to rely on the statute—either as a source of the substantive rights or as the authority for the Attorney General to commence the suit. The *Debs* Court instead decided to rely on the Constitution itself, adorned with some common law analogies, such as those allowing public officers to bring suits to remove public nuisances. It was only in the late 1890s, after *Debs,* that the Supreme Court had occasion to review the congressional grant of authority to the Attorney General to commence injunctive proceedings under the Sherman Act.[22] Of course, with *Debs* on the books there could be little doubt about the validity of that grant of authority.

Today the question remains whether it is necessary to have congressional authorization for the Attorney General to commence injunctive suits on behalf of the United States—that part of *Debs* holding congressional action unnecessary is of questionable precedential value.[23] But there is no doubt that with congressional authorization the officer model may be used. This much was left by the antitrust cases at the turn of the century, and the fact that legitimation ultimately rested on *Debs* soon dropped out of sight. There is now a strong tradition in America of using the officer model in injunctive litigation, and the civil rights movement capitalized on that tradition, often in the most striking way.

Congress's first response to the imperative of racial equality entailed in *Brown* was not to enunciate substantive rights, but rather to authorize the Attorney General to bring injunctive suits to implement the Fifteenth Amendment. This occurred in the Civil Rights Act of 1957.[24] The very next congressional initiative, the Civil Rights Act of 1960, was in large part intended to perfect the Attorney General's injunctive weaponry on behalf of voting rights.[25] In each of the subsequent civil rights acts, those of 1964[26] and 1968,[27] the pattern was repeated; the Attorney General was authorized to initiate injunctive suits to enforce a wide range of rights—public accommodations (e.g., restaurants), state facilities (e.g., parks), public schools, employment, and housing. And I have the impression that this practice—which makes the Attorney General the familiar injunctive plaintiff—has been the impetus for extending the officer model to other types of injunctive suits such as those involving trade practices, the environment, mental hospitals, and prisons.

Owing in large part to the special credibility and resources available to the Attorney General, this innovation has had important and far-reaching consequences for civil rights litigation (and for the Executive Branch). The Attorney General has been able to develop doctrine, launch suits, persuade judges, and monitor performance in a way that the citizen-plaintiff could not. It is important to note, however, that this incorporation of the officer model into the injunctive process has not been preemptive. The civil rights acts did not foreclose the private suit (though in the early 1970s, with respect to employment, legislation was proposed to that effect, and ultimately the Executive's power to sue was transferred from the Attorney General to the EEOC).[28] The result is an amalgamation—officer and citizen models coexist.

Sometimes this coexistence is more formal than real. I have in mind the structural injunction, in which Executive participation is often decisive. The power of the Executive derives from the special dependency of court and citizen in the structural context. In part the dependency stems from special evidentiary problems in the issuance phase—more than a few isolated incidents are needed before a point can be made about structure, before a judge is likely to be persuaded that he should undertake so ambitious a project as reconstructing an ongoing institution. The dependency also stems from the intractable problems of policing performance in the structural context. It takes resources as significant as those of the Department of Justice to conduct regular inspections and to evaluate the periodic reports that are usually required of the defendant in the structural context.

Since the power of the Executive derives from a dependency, and that dependency derives from needs endemic to the remedial enterprise, the power is not easily curtailed. Decentralization is not easily restored. The special needs of the structural context may to some extent be met by greater reliance on institutional litigators (e.g., the NAACP Legal Defense Fund). In the Republican years (1969–77)—when the courts could no longer count on the Department of Justice—these private institutions achieved a new importance. Even more striking has been the improvisation of the trial judges who sought to create new agencies (e.g., Human Rights Councils, special masters) to meet the special needs of structural reform; these agencies are charged with policing performance and making proposals for framing and modifying the decree.[29]

It should be noted that neither the increased role of the institutional litigator nor the emergence of these judge-created agencies returned the power of initiation to the citizen, at least not to the degree that it existed under the property injunction. Furthermore, the pluralism of the traditional regime will be achieved only if institutional litigators and judge-created agencies remain truly independent—as independent as the individual citizen.

2. The Power of Decision

Under the classical view, there was little point in distinguishing between the issuance and enforcement phases of the injunctive process—in both, the decisional authority was the judge. This was as true of the labor injunction as it was of the property injunction; indeed the 1896 presidential campaign slogan raised in protest against *Debs,* "Government by Injunction," was in essence a protest against government by the judiciary. The same was true of the anti-Progressivism injunction. But recent developments, some statutory, others constitutional, have complicated the picture. Today a complete account of the allocative scheme governing the power to decide must once again distinguish between the enforcement and issuance phases.

In the issuance phase, where the court promulgates the standard of conduct, the decisional authority is the judge. The uniqueness of this allocation is hard to gauge. For the reparative injunction the uniqueness is undeniable; the correct comparison is with the damage action, where the primary decisional agency has been the jury. Structural injunctions have no ready standard of comparison, and the uniqueness might be thought to derive as much from the nature of the enterprise as the decisional agency. With the preventive injunction, commentators have stressed the uniqueness of the decisional agency because they have used a false standard of comparison. The comparison has been made to the jury—the primary decisional agency in damage actions or criminal prosecutions. I have maintained, however, that the preventive injunction should be compared not with the damage award or judgment of conviction, but rather with the liability rule or criminal prohibition. Viewed from that perspective, the decisional authority for preventive injunctions appears less unique.

Today the promulgation of criminal prohibitions is viewed as a legislative task. But this was not true of most of our history. Common law crimes prevailed in most of the states well into the twentieth century and under that regime the criminal prohibitions were promulgated by judges. The common law system for federal crimes ended at an early point in our history, and in the federal domain statutes have predominated. But the federal domain has never occupied a pivotal conceptual position in the American criminal law system; up to now, criminal law has largely been the work of the states. In any event, many of the federal statutes gave a centrality to judges, calling upon them to define amorphous concepts (e.g., a conspiracy to defraud the United States) in order to establish the standards of conduct. The similarity of injunctions to liability rules is thus even clearer because judges have always been the primary authority for promulgating those standards.

In recent years the legislature has not only played an increasingly important role in setting liability rules and criminal prohibitions, but has also emerged in the injunctive process. This is true even in the civil rights domain. From 1954 to 1964, the civil rights injunction was almost exclusively the work of the judges, implementing the grand generalities of the Fourteenth and Fifteenth Amendments. But starting with the Civil Rights Act of 1964, dealing with public accommodations, public facilities, and private employment, and the Civil Rights Act of 1968, dealing with private housing, the civil rights injunction has had a legislative umbrella. The legislative commands have been cast in the most general terms (e.g., do not discriminate on the basis of race), and the leeway of the judiciary in fashioning the substantive rules of conduct has been considerable. Under this institutional arrangement, which is not by any means confined to civil rights, but is found throughout our legal system, the judiciary is not the exclusive decisional agency. It is a coordinate agency, exercising power delegated to it by the legislature.[30]

Looking at the injunctive process from the enforcement perspective, the proper standard of comparison is the jury. The question whether an individual violated a criminal prohibition or a liability rule is, as a formal matter, generally allocated to the jury, and that is the type of question to be resolved in the enforcement proceeding—did the defendant violate the injunction? Historically—in the era of *Debs* and *Ex parte Young*—that question was allocated to the judge. Two developments have modified that allocative scheme and have introduced the jury into the enforcement phase. One has been specific legislative enactments guaranteeing the trial by jury, some in response to the early experience with the labor and anti-Progressivism injunctions, and others as integral parts of the statutes authorizing civil rights injunctions. The second development has been *Bloom* v. *Illinois* (1968).[31] There the Supreme Court held that criminal contempt was to be included in the constitutional category of "crimes" or "criminal proceedings," thereby guaranteeing trial by jury in all criminal contempts in which the punishment was not petty—imprisonment for more than six months.

I believe, then, that even in the enforcement phase allocation of the decisional authority is not as unique as it was previously: the jury has been introduced. Differences nevertheless persist, and they should be carefully delineated. (1) For purposes of applying the *Bloom* rule in the criminal context, the severity of the punishment is determined on the basis of the maximum the judge is *authorized* to impose. In the injunctive context, the determining factor for "severity" is punishment *actually* imposed. This rule in effect gives the judge the power to settle for an imprisonment of less than six months as a means of avoiding the vagaries of a jury trial and the attendant risk of nullification. (2) In the criminal system, all fines in excess of $500 are serious. In the injunctive process the seriousness of a fine is not determined on an absolute basis, but rather must reflect the financial resources of the contemnor. *Muniz* v. *Hoffman* (1975)[32] introduced this principle of progressivity; it held that $10,000 for a union was not "severe." (3) The jury has remained out of the enforcement phase when the sanction is civil contempt rather than criminal contempt, regardless of whether the civil contempt takes the form of a conditional order (jail until compliance) or a compensatory-damage award.

Having deployed this analytic distinction between the issuance and the enforcement phases, we must not let it obscure the underlying reality: the centrality of the judge in the injunctive process. The judge is the primary decisional agency: this is the theme that unites both phases. The legislature may play a role in the issuance phase, but it is essentially one of delegator of authority. The jury might play a role in the enforcement phase, but the judge has the power to insulate his decision from jury review by settling for civil contempt or for a criminal contempt sanction (e.g., five months in prison) that might be legally deemed "petty" when in truth it is severe. The injunctive process should then be seen as *concentrating* or *fusing* the decisional power in the judge; it represents the antithesis of separation of powers.

It should also be emphasized that this concentrated or fused power is *decentralized*. The power is not allocated to the judiciary as much as it is allocated to the multitude of individual trial judges. As *Brown* II teaches, they are our chancellors. Of course, the trial judges are related to one another through a judicial hierarchy, a system of appeals, but that hierarchy is not strong enough to produce centralization.[33] For one thing, the trial judges—at least in the federal system—tend to view themselves as independent, autonomous decisional centers. As noted before, this might be due to the fact that each has an independent commission derived from the same appointing authority. Appellate judges have the power to reverse, but they do not have the usual hierarchical powers—to discharge, to promote, to determine compensation. Second, the trial judges' autonomous self-image is accommodated and reinforced by the grand generalities of the law they are called on to implement. The substantive standards embodied in the Constitution (no state shall deny equal protection of the laws) or statute (no discrimination on the basis of race) enhance the autonomy of each authoritative decision-maker. The same is true in the enforcement sphere. Third, certain well-established appellate doctrines insulate the trial judges from rigorous review by the hierarchically superior courts. For example, trial court findings of fact are protected by a clearly erroneous standard, and their mixed judgments of law and fact are usually protected by an abuse-of-discretion standard. Doctrines of discretion, so pervasive in injunctive litigation, contribute to the decentralization of decision-making authority; they may be the functional equivalent of the leeway allowed the jury[34] and result in the same degree of decentralization introduced by the jury.

The decisional authority in the injunctive process is not

only concentrated and decentralized; it is also peculiarly personalized. The recipient of the injunctive power is a person, in contrast to other recipients of nondemocratically controlled power, such as the jury—a group that in effect requires facelessness for membership and that exists for one discrete event of limited duration (a trial). The issuance or enforcement of an injunction becomes an expression of a person, as much as it is an expression of an office, and represents a striking instance of the personification of the law—when we speak of the decisional authority in the injunctive process we often talk not of *the law* or even of *the court,* but of Judge Johnson or Judge Garrity.[35]

Personification stems not only from the individual character of the recipient of power, but also from the fact that the power is both concentrated and decentralized. These features are inherent to the injunction, and thus personification can be expected in all types of injunctions. With the structural injunction, however, there is an additional factor that makes the personification even more pronounced—the judge maintains a continuous relationship with the institution over a significant period of time. There is no easy, one-shot method of reconstructing an institution; a series of interventions are inevitable, for the defendants' performance must be evaluated, and new directions issued, time and time again. Structural injunctions entail a process of continuous interaction, and that has the effect of further projecting the person rather than the office.

3. The Hearing Itself

Two types of injunctions—preliminary injunctions and temporary restraining orders—do violence to the norms that generally govern judicial behavior. Preliminary injunctions may be issued after a truncated presentation of the facts and law. The ordinary opportunities for discovery may be curtailed. The rules of evidence (such as the hearsay rule) may be abandoned;

heavy reliance is likely to be placed on documents rather than on live testimony to establish a factual point; the ordinary opportunities for cross-examination are curtailed; and often the judge must decide without adequate opportunity to study either the law or the facts. Temporary restraining orders are procedurally one degree—one significant degree—more irregular: they may be issued even without notice to the other side.

Interlocutory injunctions thus abrogate or severely modify the conception of a hearing that permeates the rest of the judicial system.[36] This uniqueness should be acknowledged,[37] and yet at the same time, one must avoid the danger of generalizing: preliminary injunctions and temporary restraining orders are very special legal instruments designed to preserve the status quo pending a judicial determination of the underlying controversy (in which the plaintiff may be seeking damages rather than an injunction). By definition interlocutory injunctions are of limited duration, and the violation of the usual procedural norms occurs in the name of preserving the opportunity to have a claim adjudicated. They are preservative of the right to have a claim heard by a court. The ordinary injunction, the final or permanent injunction, does not make the same kind of demand for expedition. The issuance of those injunctions must be preceded by a hearing and one that generally conforms to the standard procedural norms. Accordingly, when the focus is on final rather than interlocutory injunctions, the nature of the hearing preceding issuance is not a source of uniqueness for injunctions.

Turning to the enforcement phase, there are two aspects of the hearing that do introduce elements of uniqueness. The first is the rule of *Walker* v. *City of Birmingham,*[38] which denies the criminal contemnor the right to contest the constitutional validity of the outstanding decree. To be more precise, *Walker* held that it was not denial of due process for a state to foreclose a constitutional challenge to a restraining order in a criminal contempt proceeding where the restraining order was not patently invalid and where the contemnor had not moved to dissolve the restraining order before disobeying. Of course, courts are free to adopt a contrary rule; *Walker* only held that they were not constitutionally obliged to. More radically, the *Walker* rule could be flatly repudiated as being inconsistent with a basic precept of our legal system—prohibiting the imposition of sanction without an adequate opportunity to contest the constitutional validity of the underlying rule of conduct. (It is ex parte restraining orders, we should remember, that *Walker* galvanizes.)[39] But until the day comes that *Walker* is repudiated or made unavailing, we must recognize that the limitation on the defenses that could be tendered in a criminal contempt hearing is a source of uniqueness. *Walker* introduces a radical incompleteness to the criminal contempt hearing.

A second, and more subtle, distortion is introduced by the nature of the issue posed in an enforcement proceeding— whether the defendant violated the outstanding decree. In the issuance proceeding (for a final injunction) the hearing is structured on the contest model, one that is prevalent throughout all American procedure: two parties vying against one another, with the judge as an impartial umpire.[40] Once we enter the enforcement phase, however, it is likely that the triadic structure will collapse, or at least get blurred, and realignment will occur, with the judge and plaintiff now aligned against the defendant.

In criminal contempt this realignment occurs at a formal level: the judge is invested with the power of initiation; he makes the prosecutorial decision. In all contempts it is likely to arise on a practical level, given the very nature of the charge— that the defendant defied the judge's decree. In the adjudication of such a charge, it is unrealistic to expect the judge to maintain his umpireal pose in all its purity; he may be indifferent to the question of the defendant's innocence, but he has more than the usual investment in obtaining compliance with the standard of conduct. It is *his* decree. And of course, to the extent that there is not one enforcement proceeding, but an endless series of them, as is typically the case in the structural context,[41] the problem is compounded and the realignment all the more pronounced. The defendant has been found in noncompliance several times, and thus the judge is not likely to approach the question of the defendant's innocence unpredisposed; at the same time the judge's investment in the standard of conduct has increased through the very process of issuing a series of supplemental decrees. It is not surprising to learn that judges engaged in implementing structural decrees have special difficulty in maintaining their distance from the plaintiffs and the adjunct agencies used to implement the decree (e.g., amici curiae, special masters, the Department of Justice). The triadic structure is all but gone.

This realignment is not without parallels in either the damage or criminal system, once liability or guilt is established and the question is one of sanction.[42] Moreover, this triadic structure can be restored to some degree by using different judges in the issuance and enforcement phases; in fact, this has been constitutionally mandated in direct contempts (where the disobedience occurs in the presence of the court, such as the disruption of a trial).[43] The effectiveness of this proposal, admittedly, is limited by collegial ties and institutional identification, and, in any event, it may entail a loss of specialized knowledge (viewed as a form of expertise). When the same judge is retained for both issuance and enforcement phases, he can bring his familiarity with the terms and purposes of the decree to bear on the issues of enforcement, determining whether there was a violation and what the sanction should be. Ironically, this specialized knowledge is all the more important in the context of a structural decree, and yet that is the context in which the greatest strain is placed on the judge's umpireal posture—he must direct or manage the reconstruction of an on-going social institution.

C. The Sanctioning System

I have maintained that the preventive injunction might profit-ably be analyzed by comparing it to a liability rule or criminal prohibition, since all are preventive instruments. I would now like to look at the sanctions attached to the latter two legal in-struments—taken as ideal types—in order to provide a frame-work for understanding the general structure of injunctive sanctions and to determine their uniqueness.

Both liability rules and criminal prohibitions operate through deterrence: both acknowledge the risk of disobedience to the underlying command or rule of conduct and threaten to impose sanctions upon the violator. The critical difference lies in the level of the sanctions. With a liability rule, the sanctions are set at the level of costs to the victim,[44] thereby causing the perpe-trator to internalize the costs of his action. With a criminal prohibition, the sanctions are set at a higher level, sufficient not only to bring the costs of the damage caused the victim to bear on the perpetrator, but to stop the proscribed conduct alto-gether.

To mark a distinction between the ambitions of criminal prohibitions and liability rules is not to ignore some counter-vailing examples—laws today called criminal that have no greater ambition than liability rules, and vice versa. My concern is with ideal types; the categories take their meaning from core examples, which draw a distinction between the laws against murder, assault, and theft on the one hand and the laws of accidents on the other. Nor is this account contradicted by the fact that in some instances, particularly in the realm of property, the practical effect of a criminal prohibition may be to force the would-be perpetrator to bargain with the would-be victim. The proscribed conduct might be described in such a way as to make the prohibition vitally dependent on the absence of the victim's consent; a prohibition against theft, for example, does not prohibit taking another's property, but rather taking it without the owner's consent.[45] Finally, it should be clear that this distinction between the two sanctioning systems is not undermined by the fact that on occasion the criminal prohibition may fail, that in spite of the threat of sanction, an individual may decide to violate the rule of conduct (because, for example, he estimates that the likely gain is sufficient to warrant the probable sanction). This contingency does not deny the ambition of a criminal prohibition; it only acknowledges that at times the ambition may go unfulfilled.

In terms of this framework, the sanctioning system of the classic injunction, the preventive injunction, can be seen to resemble that of the criminal prohibition.[46] In issuing a preventive injunction the court promulgates a rule of conduct and also (implicitly) threatens to impose sanctions—jail or fine— for a violation; and what is more to the point, the level of the sanctions is not tied to the level of damages caused. The sanctions *might* be set at a level sufficient to discourage the individual defendant from ever violating this injunction again (the deterrence is specific in terms of the injunction and the individual—and hence I refer to it as double-specific deterrence), or to discourage this individual from violating any other injunction issued by the court (individual-specific deterrence), to discourage any other addressee of this injunction from violating it (injunction-specific deterrence), or to discourage anyone from violating any other injunction that might be issued by the court (general deterrence). In all these cases—all instances of criminal contempt—the aim is not simply to internalize the costs to the victim but to stop the prohibited act or to enhance the power of the court to stop acts that it might prohibit. Of

course, as with criminal prohibitions, on occasion the ambition
of the preventive injunction may go unfulfilled. To state the
obvious, an injunction can be violated. The rule of *Walker* v.
City of Birmingham—denying a criminal contemnor the right
to contest the constitutional validity of the injunction—may
strengthen the threat of punishment by enhancing the certainty
of infliction, but it does not guarantee that the threat will be
successful in preventing the proscribed conduct.

This account accurately captures the criminal contempt sanction; it is roughly analogous to the sanctioning system of the
criminal law. But we must also consider civil contempt. What
is so curious about civil contempt, and thus the injunctive sanctioning system, is that civil contempt consists of two quite distinct strands, each pushing in an opposite direction. One strand,
the conditional order, pushes the injunction toward the criminal
regime, and the other, the compensatory damage award, pushes
it toward the tort regime.

The most common form of civil contempt is the conditional
order: the injunction prohibits the defendant from doing X
(e.g., dumping waste in the river), the defendant does X once
(e.g., he dumps one load in the river), and, as a form of civil
contempt, the defendant is jailed until he stops doing X or until
the court is thoroughly satisfied through promises, etc. that he
will not do X. Though called civil, this form of contempt is a
variant of double-specific deterrence: its ambition is to prevent
this particular individual from violating this particular injunction again, and the court applies whatever pressure is necessary
to bring about the result. The uniqueness of conditional-order
contempt lies in its refinement. The conditional order is a more
calibrated form of specific deterrence than is available in the
criminal prosecution (or in criminal contempt): the judge need
not rely on his estimate of the probable impact of a certain
quantum of punishment on an individual's future behavior.
After one violation, the burden is cast on the contemnor to

assure the judge of the likelihood of his compliance in the future.[47]

The other form of civil contempt, an order requiring the contemnor to pay the victim damages as compensation, makes the injunction seem more like a liability rule than like a criminal prohibition. But such a reductionism would be incorrect. The preventive injunction is like a mini-criminal statute, though individuated, decentralized, and judge-issued. As long as the criminal contempt sanction remains available (and it does even if civil contempt is in fact utilized, either in its compensatory or conditional guise), the injunction will be viewed as having more stringent ambitions than a liability rule. In gauging deterrent effect, what is crucial is the expected sanction (multiplied by the probability of imposition), and that must include the whole range of sanctions possible, high and low.

Of course, the formal availability of a strong (criminal-like) sanction may be impeached by a declaration of the judge that disobedience will be met only with an award of compensatory damages or by practices to a like effect. But such declarations are rare indeed, and the award of compensatory damages as the sole or exclusive sanction has not been sufficiently pervasive to alter the conception of an injunction as a criminal prohibition. We often decry the "softness" of the judicially imposed contempt sanction, but that complaint has its counterpart in the evaluation of the criminal system as well.

Our analysis thus far—suggesting that the injunction should be viewed as a mini-criminal statute—holds for the preventive injunction. The reparative injunction uses the same sanctioning system, yet the analogy with the criminal statute collapses because the reparative injunction seeks to undo the effects of a past wrong and thus is more like an in-kind damage judgment. Contempt in the reparative context is analogous to using criminal sanctions to collect damage judgments (rather than the seizure and sale of assets—an enforcement mechanism that is awkward[48] since we are dealing with compensation in kind).

With the structural injunction the analogy to the deterrence system of the criminal law is even less successful. For structural injunctions the sanctioning system primarily consists of supplemental decrees, not contempt, either civil or criminal. The usual scenario in the structural context is for the judge to issue a decree (perhaps embodying a plan formulated by the defendant), to be confronted with disobedience, and then not to inflict contempt but to grant a motion for supplemental relief. Then the cycle repeats itself. In each cycle of the supplemental relief process the remedial obligation is defined with greater and greater specificity. Ultimately, after many cycles of supplemental decrees, the ordinary contempt sanctions may become realistically available, but the point to emphasize is that it is *only* then—only at the end of a series—that the threat of contempt becomes credible.

The gradualism of the structural sanctioning system might be attributable to political considerations (such as a desire to "go slow" so as to build wide popular support for the remedial enterprise). In a similar vein, it might be said that it reflects an ambivalence toward the underlying decree. I suspect, however, that the gradualism has deeper roots—uncertainties in the goal to be achieved (e.g., what is a "unitary nonracial" school system) or shortcomings in our knowledge and ability to restructure ongoing institutions—and thus is less tractable. The gradualism stems from the very nature of the remedial enterprise.

The unique sanctioning system of structural decrees coalesces with another characteristic identified earlier—the fact that structural decrees are not preventive. A structural decree—one of the most distinctive legacies of the civil rights experience—should not be viewed as an instrument seeking to prevent a future wrong through deterrence. Rather, it should be viewed as a means of initiating a relationship between a court and a social institution.[49] The issuance of the injunction is not so much a coercive act, such as issuing a command, as it is a declaration that henceforth the court will *direct* or *manage* the reconstruction of the social institution, in order to bring it into conformity with the Constitution. The first ploy of any manager is to induce collaboration; authoritative directives are reserved as a last resort.

III

The Remedial Hierarchy

In the previous chapter I inquired into the nature of the injunction and turned to other remedies to locate the unique contributions made by the injunction. I now wish to examine the formal relationship between the injunction and other remedies—to describe that relationship and, even more, to see whether it can be justified.

I begin with the legacy of the property injunction—the view that in our legal system the relationship among remedies is hierarchical and that in this hierarchy the injunction is disfavored, ranked low. This hierarchical relationship and the subordination of the injunction is, we recall, primarily the handiwork of the irreparable injury requirement. That requirement makes the issuance of an injunction conditional upon a showing that the plaintiff has no alternative remedy that will adequately repair his injury. Operationally this means that as a general proposition the plaintiff is remitted to some remedy other than an injunction unless he can show that his noninjunctive remedies are inadequate.

There are, to be certain, ambiguities latent in the doctrine. For one thing, inadequacy is not a dichotomous quality, but rather permits of degree, and yet the degree required is never specified. It is not clear how inadequate—whether greatly or slightly—the alternative remedy must be before an entitlement to an injunction is established. Second, there is uncertainty as to which types of inadequacies are to count for the purpose of applying the test. What about the retrospective nature of the damage action, the interposition of the jury, or the future financial unresponsiveness of the defendant? From one standpoint —that of the plaintiff seeking the strongest safeguard of his rights—they are viewed as inadequacies; not so from a more disinterested perspective. Counting the retrospective nature of the damage award as an inadequacy would require a reordering of the hierarchy that would undermine the very doctrine being applied, for that defect is always present. The interposition of the jury also might not count as a defect because the Constitution requires it to be viewed as a virtue. And it might even be argued that the likely financial unresponsiveness of the defendant should not count, because it would strain institutional resources by placing an excessive front load on each individual injunctive lawsuit if an evidentiary inquiry into the present and future financial resources of the defendant were permitted. Third, ambiguities inhere in the irreparable injury requirement because it is not clear which alternative remedies must be shown to be inadequate before the injunction is available. Is it just the damage action or criminal prosecution, or is it also, as the Supreme Court has recently suggested,[1] the criminal defense, habeas corpus, removal proceedings, change of venue, disciplinary proceedings, and even appellate review?

These ambiguities permit considerable manipulation of the doctrine. Yet I am concerned with the unmistakable general effect of the doctrine: it creates a remedial hierarchy and relegates the injunction to a subordinate place in that hierarchy. The inadequacy of alternative remedies must be demonstrated before the injunction can be utilized, but there is no reciprocal requirement on those alternative remedies. The plaintiff in a damage action or a criminal prosecution, for example, need not establish the inadequacy of the injunction before those remedies come available.

This hierarchical relationship among remedies is not exclu-

sively the product of the irreparable injury requirement. It
derives from several other doctrines as well, although they are
of less general scope. One is the prior restraint doctrine, applicable to injunctions against speech. This doctrine does not
altogether preclude the issuance of an injunction aimed at
speech, but rather places a burden on such injunctions that is
not placed on other legal instruments aimed at speech, such
as damage judgments, criminal convictions, liability rules, or
criminal prohibitions. The doctrine contemplates two standards—one for injunctions and another for all other legal
instruments. For the injunction to issue, the speech not only
must be unprotected but also must be so in some dramatic,
clear, and special way, as exemplified in the troop movement
paradigm, which Chief Justice Hughes suggested in *Near* v.
Minnesota, the basic precedent for the prior restraint doctrine:
an injunction against speech might be allowed if and only if the
speech sought to be prevented was as *clearly* unprotected as that
disclosing the movements of troops at time of war.[2] Speech falling short of that standard but nonetheless constitutionally unprotected might be the subject of other legal instruments, such
as a criminal prohibition or prosecution, but not the injunction.
In our culture the prior restraint doctrine is tied to the constitutional guarantee of freedom of speech, but the same sentiment
is expressed in the traditional equitable maxim that equity will
not enjoin a libel.

Another traditional maxim, to the effect that equity will not
enjoin a crime, also might be viewed as a subordinating doctrine. When the conduct sought to be restrained is also proscribed by a criminal prohibition, the court will not issue an
injunction even if there be a coordinate source of illegality (e.g.,
a civil nuisance law), unless the plaintiff demonstrates the
inadequacy of the criminal remedy. A preference is thereby
expressed for the criminal remedy.

Finally, there is the doctrine that transformed the usual

province of the classical injunction—the property injunction—
into an exclusive domain: equity will intervene only to protect
property rights. The injunctive plaintiff is put to the task of
convincing the court that the interest he wishes to protect is a
property interest; that hurdle is not encountered in the request
for other remedies, the protective scope of which is, as evi-
denced by the early assault cases, as broad as the totality of
human interests.

In identifying these doctrines separately—irreparable injury, prior restraint, not enjoining a crime, and protecting only
property rights—we should not lose sight of the fact that all
may be invoked in the same case. Indeed, in *Debs* all these
subordinating doctrines seem to have converged, making the
issuance of an injunction that much more exceptional. The
conduct enjoined in *Debs* was arguably the subject of federal
and state criminal statutes, and in fact Eugene Debs and other
strike leaders were not only held in criminal contempt but also
criminally prosecuted for restraining trade in violation of the
Sherman Antitrust Act.[3] (The Court deemed the criminal
prosecution inadequate because of the risk of jury nullification,
failing to consider the very real possibility that the chance of
jury nullification was a right Debs was entitled to, not a defect
of the criminal remedy.) The prior restraint principle was also
flouted, for the injunction prohibited Debs from speaking to or
in any way addressing the strikers. The speech issue was not
discussed in the opinion of the Supreme Court, and indeed that
particular provision of the injunction is not printed in *U.S.
Reports*, but the anti–free speech quality of the *Debs* injunction
was a focal point of criticism by the federal commission subse-
quently convened to examine the Pullman Strike and its repres-
sion.[4] The property interest requirement was in fact discussed
by the Court in *Debs,* but the strained quality of the means
chosen to meet that requirement—to point to the property interest the United States had in the mails—was apparent to all.

The last of the subordinating doctrines—the one that confines injunctions to the protection of property interests—need
not detain us. It is so devoid of justification—indeed I cannot
think of a single argument in support of it—that we may treat
it as having already been repudiated. No one takes it seriously.
The only point worth noting is that the repudiation was so long
in coming, in fact was not finally accomplished until the civil
rights injunction became firmly rooted, until it became clear
that we were not prepared to live without *Brown*. The classic
citation for repudiation, *Kenyon* v. *City of Chicopee*[5], is a 1946
case, one in which Jehovah's Witnesses sought an injunction
against authorities interfering with the distribution of hand-
bills. The Massachusetts court put the doctrine to rest by
capitalizing on the emerging consensus on the importance of
constitutionally based human rights, a consensus that ultimately
provided the substantive foundations for the civil rights injunction and *Brown*. The court reasoned: "If equity would
safeguard their right to sell bananas it ought to be at least
equally solicitous of their personal liberties guaranteed by the
Constitution."[6]

The other subordinating doctrines are of continuing vitality.
This is obviously true of the prior restraint doctrine, which
seems to be invoked with increasing frequency. I also think the
equity-does-not-enjoin-a-crime doctrine and the more generalized irreparable injury requirement are alive and well. They
continue to be invoked and affirmed. Indeed, the irreparable
injury requirement—the principal object of my attack—seems
to have received a new lease on life in *Douglas* v. *City of Jeannette*,[7] another 1940s case involving the Jehovah's Witnesses,
and it was reinvigorated with a vengeance by a line of cases that
begins in 1971 with *Younger* v. *Harris*.[8]

The subordinating doctrines can be traced back to English
Chancery practice, and thus it is not surprising that they were
primarily addressed to the traditional form of the injunction,

the preventive one. Some of the doctrines, such as prior restraint, are confined to those injunctions. Other of the subordinating doctrines, however, have not been so confined, but have been applied to the newer types of injunctions, those linked to the more recent civil rights experience. The irreparable injury requirement has, for example, been applied to the structural injunction in *O'Shea* v. *Littleton*.[9] The plaintiffs there sought, in part, an injunction against the state judges prohibiting them from determining bail on a mass basis and from discriminating on the basis of race in sentencing; they were in effect seeking a reorganization of the criminal justice system in Cairo, Illinois. The Supreme Court denied relief and rationalized this result in terms of the irreparable injury requirement. The plaintiffs had not established the requisite irreparable injury, the Court complained; they had not demonstrated the inadequacy of a host of alternative remedies—damage actions, criminal prosecutions, change of venue, removal proceedings, appellate review, habeas corpus.

I recognize the usual problem of the "gap": the subordinating doctrines express formal rules, and there may be a gap between actual judicial practice and formal rules. Indeed, it was the discordance between doctrine and practice that fueled this intellectual enterprise: doctrines required subordination, and yet the injunction was the primary remedy. In truth the civil rights plaintiff was not put to the task of establishing the inadequacy of alternative remedies, and that led me to inquire into the justification of the doctrine. On the other hand, the existence of this "gap" between doctrine and practice in the civil rights area does not moot this inquiry—far from it.

First, the durability of the civil rights experience is in doubt, as *Littleton*—a 1974 decision—so explicitly reveals. The Supreme Court now seems bent on reversing the practice of resorting to the injunction as a primary remedy and is narrowly circumscribing, if not cutting back on, the injunction even in the civil rights domain. Second, there is a question of the generality of the civil rights experience. Even at its peak, the civil rights practice did not prevail across the legal system. In some domains the ascendancy of the injunction was far from assured even as a practical matter. Third, even if there were no doubts about the durability or generality of the civil rights experience, an inquiry into the justification of doctrine—arguably discordant with practice—would still remain vital. For the notion of remedial hierarchy, even as a purely formal construct, might well have psychological and normative significance. The construct might well *influence* how the profession actually views or thinks about a practice (the psychological significance), and, more importantly, it might determine the *legitimacy* of a practice (the normative significance). Indeed, one could view this assault on the remedial hierarchy not as an attempt to modify the practice reflected in civil rights litigation, one of assigning the injunction a primary role, but rather to see whether the practice is legitimate. On questions of legitimacy, doctrine is central.

I also recognize that some might point to history to explain the remedial hierarchy and the place of the injunction in it. They might remind us of the fact that the injunction evolved as a legal instrument belonging to a system of justice—administered by the Chancellor—that was intended to be a supplementary system, to provide relief when the common law system failed. I for one am not fully satisfied with this familiar historical account, even taken as an explanation of the remedial hierarchy. (1) This account does not explain the continuing vitality of the doctrine when the institutional arrangements that gave rise to it have disappeared through, for example, the merger of the legal and equitable forums. (2) It does not explain why doctrine such as irreparable injury today applies to injunctions, but not to other remedies originally administered by equity, such as those relating to mortgages and trusts. (3) Nor does it explain why the injunction became the exclusive property of the Chancellor, the supplementary system, rather than the primary system—the common law system. Professor Hazeltine's research shows that the "new tribunal [Chancery] built partly on the older practice of the common law" and that the early (i.e., fourteenth century) common law courts issued what we would today call injunctions (though under the labels of writ quia timet, writ of estrepement and writ of prohibition).[10] But even if I am wrong on this score, even if the familiar historical account is complete as an *explanation,* it must fail my purpose—to inquire into the *justification* of the remedial hierarchy. I am asking normative questions—whether it is *correct* to conceive of remedies in a hierarchical fashion and to assign the injunction a subordinate position in that hierarchy.

A. The Argument from Due Process

One species of injunction—interlocutory injunctions—poses a threat to the right to be heard. They enhance the risk of error and evince a disrespect for the individual by denying him the opportunity to participate in a process that will have a direct and immediate impact on his well-being. This much cannot be denied; on the other hand, it would be a mistake to generalize about all injunctions because of the special defect of interlocutory injunctions—to determine the place of the injunction on the basis of the procedural irregularity of temporary restraining orders and preliminary injunctions.

This tendency to generalize is manifest in Frankfurter and Greene, who largely built their case against the labor injunction on the basis of the evils and abuses of *interlocutory* labor injunctions. They began with *Debs* and the slogan raised against that case, "Government by Injunction"; but they never paid sufficient attention to detail—the fact that the *Debs* injunction was a temporary restraining order, issued without the slightest attempt to get the adversary to participate in the proceeding. Even less attention was paid to this detail in the Norris-La-Guardia ban. Admittedly, the special time-bounded quality of a strike often makes the interlocutory injunction decisive in the labor context; a temporary halt of a strike might break the strikers' momentum altogether or insulate the employer from pressure at his most vulnerable operating phase. But this only explains or excuses the mode of the Frankfurter and Greene analysis, the tendency to generalize from the interlocutory injunction; it does not recommend that it be followed.

This same misguided tendency to generalize has shown up more recently, this time in Justice Powell's attempt to justify the prior restraint doctrine. "The special vice of a prior restraint," he wrote, "is that communication will be suppressed, either directly or by inducing excessive caution in the speaker, *before an adequate determination* that it is unprotected by the First Amendment."[11] If the prior restraint doctrine were confined to interlocutory injunctions, that is, ones issued, as in the case of temporary restraining orders, without participation by the adversary and without the benefit of appellate review, and in any event issued prior to a full hearing on the law and the facts, where the judge must act with great haste, then Justice Powell's justification would make sense; a special concern for error costs in the First Amendment domain might compound the distaste for interlocutory injunctions that flows from due process.[12] But this process-oriented justification for the prior restraint doctrine does not make sense when the focus shifts to final injunctions. There is not the slightest reason to believe that they will be issued without "adequate determination." Indeed, if I were to make a guess, though I believe it a mistake to generalize in this fashion, I would probably have to say that in the generality of cases the determination that precedes the issuance of a final injunction is not only "adequate" but probably superior to that which generally precedes the promulgation of the truly comparable preventive ("prior") instruments, liability rules and criminal prohibitions.

I would suggest, then, that the argument from the irregular quality of the interlocutory process, whether it is based on the Due Process Clause alone or is coupled with the First Amendment, does not justify a subordination of the injunction. All it justifies is a set of restrictions on the issuance of interlocutory injunctions, as was realized in the first waves of congressional reform—the Three Judge Act of 1910 and the Clayton Act of 1914—which were primarily aimed at interlocutory injunctions (*Ex parte Young*, like *Debs*, involved an interlocutory injunction). Some of the restrictions may be formalistic: a bonding requirement, time limitations for the duration of the interlocutory injunctions, affidavits about the impossibility of giving notice and the urgency of relief, interlocutory review, increased quorum, etc. Other requirements may be more substantive.

One substantive requirement might be that the plaintiff establish a likelihood of succeeding on the ultimate merits—a requirement that is commonplace in America, but is being questioned now in England.[13] This substantive requirement might be especially stringent in the First Amendment domain, thus yielding a mini–prior restraint doctrine, that is, one tied to interlocutory injunctions: in order to get an interlocutory injunction against speech, it would have to be absolutely clear— such as is suggested by the troop movement paradigm—that the speech is unprotected. This is not to belittle the reach of the prior restraint doctrine thus reformulated. In litigation aimed at speech, the interlocutory phase is often decisive: a denial of interlocutory relief will often moot the censor's plea. This is typically the case when the censor claims the speech will reveal a "secret."[14] But this is obviously not the whole story. There are many situations in which the request for final injunctive relief survives a denial of interlocutory relief; as much is suggested by *Pittsburgh Press* itself, the case in which Justice Powell offered the process rationale, for it involved a final injunction (against sex-classified ads in newspapers). So did the other classic prior restraint precedents, such as *Organization for a Better Austin*[15] (injunction against distribution of pamphlets said to invade privacy and harass) and *Near* v. *Minnesota* itself (injunction against publication of a newspaper). In these spheres, the request for interlocutory relief is not coextensive with the request for injunctive relief. The mini–prior restraint doctrine, which I concede can be justified in process terms, is not coextensive with the traditional or more familiar prior restraint doctrine, which applies to all injunctions aimed at speech and which cannot be justified in process terms.

A concern for process might also justify an irreparable injury requirement for interlocutory injunctions: the plaintiff has to demonstrate that the defendant would cause irreparable injury unless immediately enjoined. This substantive requirement, presently found in most jurisdictions, invokes the same verbal formula that applies to final injunctions, irreparable injury. There is, however, a critical difference; in fact, as in the case of the prior restraint doctrine, it would be best to recognize two distinct irreparable injury requirements—one for interlocutory and the other for final injunctions. In the context of final injunctions the irreparable injury requirement subordinates the injunction to noninjunctive remedies; in the interlocutory context, the irreparable injury requirement subordinates the interlocutory injunction to the remedy sought at the end of the lawsuit, a remedy that might be either injunctive or noninjunctive (such as damages). In the interlocutory context, the irreparable injury requirement could be viewed as protective of the right to be heard; in the final context, it serves no such purpose.

Of course, many litigants try to use an interlocutory injunction as a substitute for a final injunction. But the appropriate response to that practice is to be wary of the request for inter-locutory injunctions, not to impose restrictions on the issuance —after a full hearing—of final injunctions that are not imposed on other remedies. Such restrictions are overbroad, and even more, they create the wrong incentive structure. Since the re-strictions would be applicable to both interlocutory and final injunctions, the litigator would have little reason to observe a distinction between the two types of injunctions—if he can get one he is likely to get the other.

The due process argument primarily stems from a concern with interlocutory injunctions, but it may be seen to have other roots. For example, as I noted earlier, the rule of *Walker* v. *City of Birmingham* introduces a radical incompleteness into a criminal contempt hearing: it denies the alleged contemnor the right to be heard on the constitutionality of the underlying decree. This curb on the right to be heard might properly be viewed as a denial of due process, but surely what follows from this view is an abrogation of the *Walker* rule, not the subordi-nation of the injunction.

A similar point could be made with the objection that stems from the breadth of a decree—that it sometimes binds persons who were not parties to the proceedings: the cure lies in restrict-ing the scope of the decree. There is, however, a more basic response that could be made and indeed must be made for many decrees—particularly of the structural variety—where the scope is not easily narrowed. The dictates of due process will be satisfied if the interests of the persons bound by the de-cree are adequately represented.[16] A structural decree trying to reform the practices of a municipal police department will invariably have an effect upon all the individual police officers, present and future; on the other hand, due process does not require that each participate in the lawsuit qua party, but rather that they be adequately represented by, say, the police chief and other supervisory personnel.[17] It would not be a denial of due process to preclude individual officers from relitigating the validity of the decree, to subject them to supplemental decrees defining their obligations with greater specificity, or, if they had sufficient notice of the decree, to impose civil (damages) and criminal sanctions (under 18 U.S.C. § 1509 or criminal contempt).

A final due process argument for subordination might be based on the collapse of the triadic hearing structure—the subtle realignment of parties and judge that is likely to occur in the enforcement phase. The threat is not to the right to be heard, but rather to the *impartiality* of the hearer. I concede that an impartial decision-maker may be required by due process, and that in some situations—such as in the structural context—it may be hard (though not impossible) to preserve the umpireal posture by using different judges in the enforcement and issuance phases. And yet it seems a mistake, and without basis in precedent,[18] to read the due process requirement of impartiality to make the contest model of adjudication a constitutional necessity, to constitutionalize the position of passive umpire. The investment a judge is likely to have in seeing that his previous orders are complied with does not seem to me the kind of bias the constitutional norm of impartiality should guard against.

B. The Argument from Institutional Preferences

1. The Jury

The relationship between the injunction and the right to trial by jury is the product of a threefold historical accident: (a) Two independent legal systems developed in England, the common law courts and Chancery, and one of them, Chancery, did not recognize a jury trial right. It could be expected that Chancery would not utilize the jury, but there is no functional explanation of why there had to be two legal systems, why the dispensation (equity) function of Chancery could not be integrated into the existing legal system. (b) The injunction was used only by the Chancery, the legal system in which there was no jury trial right. The injunction could (also) have been an instrument of the common law courts, the ones that did recognize a jury trial right. (c) The American Constitution did not aspire to create a jury trial right afresh or to expand it beyond the English bounds, but rather sought to codify the English practice as it then existed, thereby freezing into the American jury trial right the late eighteenth-century English distinction between law and equity.

I emphasize the accidental character of this relationship not to deny its reality, but rather to deny its inevitability. The relationship between the jury trial right and the injunction could be altered. The jury could be integrated into the injunctive process. This is relevant for our purposes for it means that the absence of the jury trial cannot be the defect that justifies the subordination of the injunction. If the absence of the jury were really perceived as a defect, we could integrate it into the injunctive process, and the failure to do so should not count as a reason for subordinating the injunction, but rather should be read as a sign, along with others, of an ambivalence toward the jury right.[19]

The constitutional preference for the jury is strongest in the criminal domain. There the power of the state is brought to bear on an individual for violating a governmental prohibition, and the jury—an ad hoc group of lay citizens who need not explain their decision—can be seen as tempering harsh and arbitrary laws through the power of nullification. Criminal contempt is the aspect of the injunctive process most analogous to the criminal prosecution, and, as might be expected, the critics of the injunction, such as those who attacked *Debs* and the labor injunction, focussed on criminal contempt. They argued that the injunction should be subordinated because criminal contempt abridged the jury trial right.

What the critics overlooked, however, was the possibility of integrating the jury within the criminal contempt phase of the injunctive process. This possibility was recognized by legislators, who provided for trial by jury in criminal contempt proceedings, thereby undercutting this particular argument for subordination. The legislative integration was selective, confined to certain substantive categories of injunctions, such as the labor injunction, and, much later, to the civil rights injunction. But the integration was generalized by the Supreme Court in *Bloom* v. *Illinois*, requiring a jury trial right in all criminal contempts in which the sanction was not "petty." And it does not strike me as accidental that the integration occurred at the same moment as the incorporation decision was made, that is, when the Supreme Court decided the criminal jury trial provisions were binding on the states.[20] For the incorporation decision was tantamount to an affirmation of our constitutional commitment to the criminal jury. Having made the judgment that the jury trial right was important (or "fundamental") enough to become applicable to the states, it was hard to think of a good reason why it should not be made applicable to criminal contempt.

I do not mean to suggest that the integration of the jury into the injunctive process is complete. It has been integrated into criminal contempt, but three gaps still persist, and each should be analyzed separately: (1) conditional-order civil contempt; (2) compensatory-damage civil contempt; and (3) the issuance phase.

The absence of a jury in conditional-order civil contempt is particularly troubling given my insistence that that sanction should be viewed as a specially calibrated form of specific deterrence. As an instrument of deterrence that puts liberty in jeopardy, conditional-order civil contempt, like criminal contempt, should invoke the constitutional preference for the criminal jury; I do not understand why the specificity of the deterrent effect should reduce the need for the jury. On the other hand, the appropriate response to this gap, as with criminal contempt, is not the subordination of the injunction. Rather, the appropriate response is to integrate the jury into conditional-order civil contempt. The jury would, for example, decide whether the alleged contemnor violated the decree, whether he should be imprisoned until future compliance, and whether he has brought himself into compliance.[21] The jury's role would be roughly analogous to its role in criminal contempt, introducing that same risk of nullification, though there would be an additional problem of working out the definition of "petty" since the sanction is not finite.

Admittedly, the Supreme Court might have more difficulty in achieving the integration of the jury into conditional-order civil contempt. The constitutional text is not as congenial as it was for criminal contempt. It is harder to fit conditional-order civil contempt into the constitutional categories of "crime" or "criminal prosecution." But if the constitutional preference for the jury is strong enough to justify subordination of the injunction, then ways could be found to overcome the labels, the word "civil."[22] The Court could declare that the traditional categorization of conditional-order contempt as a form of civil contempt was mistaken—from the functional perspective it should be seen as a variety of criminal contempt. Literalism would be eschewed in favor of functionalism. Alternatively, the reform could be predicated on the Due Process Clause directly, thereby avoiding the categorization problems that arise from the words "crimes" or "criminal prosecution." Or, conceivably, a notion of supervisory powers could be utilized when the contempt processes of the federal courts are at issue.

Moreover, even if these moves are unavailing, the gap need not be filled by the judiciary. As with criminal contempt, the legislature could take the initiative. In the legislative halls the historical categorization of the conditional-order contempt as a form of civil contempt would not be controlling. The legislative power over contempts may be restrained by the separation-of-powers principle, but it is hard to imagine that principle precluding this particular legislative reform. Separation of powers retains so little bite today, it is not likely to be read as prohibiting a legislative reform that can be viewed as being predicated, not on a desire to weaken judicial power, but rather on a desire to broaden the reach of individual rights that might well have a constitutional basis.

I maintain then that the jury could be integrated into conditional-order contempt, as it has been for criminal contempt. The same is true for the remaining variant of civil contempt, the compensatory-damage order. The ordinary tort or contract action amply reveals the possibility of such an integration. Moreover, there is little need to *count* on legislative initiatives to effectuate this reform. Here the constitutional text is more congenial. The Supreme Court need only note the functional equivalence between the compensatory-damage civil contempt and the ordinary tort action, and construe the introductory words of the Seventh Amendment, a "suit at common law," to embrace this form of civil contempt. Such a construction might be criticized as being ahistorical, yet it is not clear that such an objection should be decisive. It certainly was not decisive for the Supreme Court in determining, for example, the required size[23] and decisional rule of the jury (i.e., whether the jury must use a unanimity rule).[24] Nor is it clear what an historical approach would produce when, as in this instance, the historical basis of the enforcement technique seems very much in doubt. I am not certain that compensatory-damage civil contempt existed in English equity practice in 1791, nor how it could be squared with the classic maxim that equity acts in personam.[25]

Integration of the jury into the compensatory-damage civil

contempt is a distinct possibility, I would maintain; but of course the truth of the matter is that it is unlikely to materialize. We are too ambivalent toward the civil jury. In the damage area, the jury is not a preferred institution, but merely one that we are constitutionally stuck with. That is why the Seventh Amendment—the one that "guarantees" and thus commits us to the civil jury—has not been made applicable to the states (the only other provision of the Bill of Rights that has this status is the grand jury guarantee of the Fifth Amendment).[26] The point I wish to make, however, is that it would be impermissible to use the absence of the jury in compensatory-damage civil contempt as a justification for subordinating the injunction, and that point is supported rather than contradicted by the constitutional ambivalence toward the civil jury.

Finally, there is the issuance phase—does the absence of the jury here justify subordination? The structure of my argument here is the same as it was with compensatory-damage civil contempt—it comes to rest on a doubt whether the civil jury is a preferred decisional agency. There are, however, additional complications. For the possibility of integrating the jury into this phase of the injunctive process is less apparent. The jury can be easily integrated with the reparative injunction since it is like an in-kind damage judgment. But additional problems arise with the preventive injunction, and even more with the structural one. The jury would have to design the decree, and, in the structural context, continuously modify that design in light of the defendant's performance and changed conditions.

This objection to integration might be muted if a bifurcated procedure were employed—letting the jury decide whether the substantive right was violated, and letting the judge design the decree. But such a scheme would be subject to an objection that I consider to be sound, namely that it incorrectly presupposes too clear a distinction between violation and remedy. The remedy and violation are interdependent. A judgment about violation should reflect, and in fact does reflect, a judgment about remedy. Accordingly, we must confront the possibility that the jury will decide not just whether an injunction should issue, but also what its terms should be.

Such a scheme would of course put a new strain on the jury, and yet I do not regard the tasks as unmanageable. The lay status of the jury could be compensated for by fuller evidentiary presentations on the remedy; such presentations might include testimony of experts, and they could be structured and interpreted by judicial instructions. The group nature of the jury would not preclude its use in designing the decree: most statutes are drafted by committee. Admittedly, the structural decree would require a single jury to remain in existence for a long period of time—that would be an onerous burden but not an impossible one, as reference to grand jury practice reveals.

The truth of the matter is, once again, that this integration of the jury into the injunctive process will not occur; integration is even less likely to occur in the issuance phase than in compensatory-damage civil contempt (a component of the enforcement phase). The constitutional preference for the jury is at its weakest in the issuance phase. This is in part due to the fact that at issue is a second right: assuming the jury trial right is honored in the enforcement phase, as it surely is with criminal contempt, then the demand for the jury in the issuance phase is in essence a demand for a second jury. The constitutional preference for the jury is not that strong.

The weakness of the preference for the jury in the issuance phase also stems from the fact that it entails the promulgation of future standards of conduct, and in those matters there seems little demand for a jury. This is not true for reparative injunctions since the command is roughly analogous to the command to pay money damages but is true for the structural injunction, which does not have a ready comparison in traditional legal domains, where the jury is found. Its closest analog may be found in administrative law. And as for preventive injunctions, I have argued that the proper analog is not the damage action or the criminal prosecution, proceedings where the jury is traditionally found, but rather those processes—some judicial and others legislative—that precede the promulgation of liability rules and criminal prohibitions. No one suggests that these tasks be turned over to the jury.

True, injunctions are capable of greater individuation than, say, liability rules or criminal prohibitions, but I fail to see why that quality of an injunction, even if realized, provides the foundation for a jury trial claim. The claim for a jury trial does not, in my judgment, get stronger as one moves from a nonindividuated injunction (do not discriminate on the basis of race) to a highly individuated one (admit James Meredith to the University of Mississippi).[27]

Similarly, I do not believe that a preference for the jury in the issuance phase of the injunctive process can be predicated on the unique nature of the decisional agency. For the moment, I am willing to assume that the judge is a nonrepresentative decisional agency and that this nonrepresentativeness is a special source of concern with the issuance phase of the injunctive process, a source of concern not present with the criminal statute that is promulgated by a legislature. It still remains to be seen whether the jury is the proper antidote: we may not want the kind of representativeness that comes from the jury. The jury is not a representative body in the same sense that a legislature is.

The properly constituted (i.e., randomly chosen) jury panel is a representative body in the same sense that a scepter might be said to represent the sovereign—it *stands for* the public (the pictorial or ornamental sense of representation). But there is no sense in which the jury panel (and much less that much smaller group that survives excuses and challenges) can be said to *speak for* the public (the agency sense of representation) as

a legislature might.[28] This is due not just to the unanimity requirement, which could be modified, but also to the absence
of any mechanism of accountability between the public and the
jury, and the conceptual impossibility of developing such an
accountability mechanism.[29] The secrecy of the jury's delibera-
tions (the fact that it need not discuss the case in public), the
fact that the jury need not explain or justify decisions, and its
one-shot quality (i.e., the fact that a new jury is convened for
each case) preclude the development of a proper mechanism of
accountability. And these are core features of the jury. If we
tried to eliminate those features, and also abrogated the unanimity requirement, we would cease to have a jury and instead
would have created a six-to-twelve person legislature.[30] We may
prefer the legislature to the judge, and for that reason subordinate the injunction, an argument still to be considered, but we
should not let a demand for a jury be a proxy for the preference
for the legislature.

2. The Legislature

Our democratic ethos gives a preference to the more representative institutions. Juries may not be considered representative in the sense called for by democratic theory, but surely
legislatures are. The question then arises whether the subordination of the injunction may reflect this democratic preference
for the legislature.[31] The judiciary is less representative than the
legislature, and in the issuance phase, so the argument continues, the judiciary is supreme.

The irreparable injury requirement purports to be a general
requirement, one to be applied across the board to all types of
injunctive proceedings, and accordingly the justification for
that doctrine must be equally general. The representativeness
argument appears to have the requisite generality. The truth
of the matter, however, is that it cannot be successfully main-

tained in this generalized form. The argument collapses at three different points.

First, the assumption about the democratic character of the remedies given priority over the injunction can be questioned. It is overbroad. For the injunction to be subordinated to an alternative legal instrument it must be shown that the alternative does not also share the same defect; the fact that the judiciary, rather than the legislature, is the prime decisional agency in the injunctive process cannot be used as the basis for placing the injunction beneath another remedy that gives the judiciary (as opposed to the legislature) an equally primary role. From this perspective, the argument from representativeness at best subordinates the injunction to the contemporary criminal prohibition. It cannot justify subordinating the injunction to liability rules, which even in their contemporary guise are promulgated primarily by the judiciary; nor can it justify subordinating the injunction to remedies such as declaratory judgments and habeas corpus, which contemplate a comparable role for the judiciary.

Second, we can question the assumption about the role of the judiciary even in the injunctive process. That assumption is also overbroad. The property injunction, the labor injunction, and, of course, the anti-Progressivism injunction were typically issued without statutory authorization. But as we noted before,[32] the more familiar injunction today—whether it be civil rights, antitrust, or even the injunction against public employee strikes—characteristically has a legislative umbrella. In these situations there is some degree of statutory authorization, and it makes little sense to use the irreparable injury requirement (or any of the other subordinating doctrines) as a means for preserving legislative primacy. (To broaden this point even further, though I am reluctant to do so, one need only fasten on the power of the legislature to curb the injunctive proclivity of the judiciary, and read the legislative silence as an "implied authorization.")

Third, we can question the assumed preference for the more representative branch. Once again it is overbroad. If nothing more is at stake than the formulation of "public policy," as was true with the property injunction and the labor injunction, then it is fair to assume that the nonrepresentative character of the judiciary is a vice. But if the focus shifts to the civil rights injunction, and either the minority-group orientation or the constitutional basis of the substantive right, then the nonrepresentative quality of the judiciary becomes a virtue rather than a vice. Constitutional rights are supposed to be countermajoritarian, and those emanating from the Equal Protection Clause particularly so.

Admittedly, it is possible to construct a theory transforming any claim for relief—injunctive or otherwise—into a protection of "minority rights," or, given a revival of substantive due process, a protection of a constitutional liberty. That is the overriding lesson of anti-Progressivism. Curbs are surely needed. But those curbs should emanate from a substantive theory of judicial review, such as that embodied in footnote 4 of *Carolene Products,* which confines judicial activism to the protection of specific constitutional guarantees (e.g., First Amendment), the correction of conduct that interferes with the democratic processes (e.g., abridgments of the right to vote), and the protection of "discrete and insular minorities" whose welfare cannot be safely entrusted to the normal workings of democratic processes.[33] These curbs should not emanate from a view about remedies, nor should they be expressed in so broad and so indirect an instrument as the traditional irreparable injury formula. That formula generalizes the curbs across the legal system and suggests that they have a source in the remedy, when in truth they are rooted in the substantive claim.

The argument from a preference for representative institutions can thus be faulted for resting on premises that are over-broad—that the supremacy of the legislature is assured with other remedies, that injunctions are devoid of statutory authorization, and that the nonrepresentativeness of the judiciary is always an evil. The irreparable injury requirement requires premises as broad as these, and yet, as becomes evident once attention is paid to the civil rights injunction, these premises cannot be maintained with such generality. Furthermore, once the premises are carved back to their proper reach, an even deeper and more intractable logical problem of the representativeness argument emerges, and that is its self-defeating quality: when the argument justifying subordination has its greatest force, the ordinary subordinating doctrines—such as the irreparable injury requirement—are inapplicable.

The representativeness argument has its greatest force when the legislature has not spoken or has decided not to enact a criminal prohibition or liability rule that might render the defendant's conduct unlawful. This is the situation in which it would be most appropriate to argue that the injunction should not issue, because otherwise the judiciary would be usurping the legislative task. But this is the very situation in which the irreparable injury requirement (or the equity-does-not-enjoin-a-crime maxim) would *not* be a ban on the issuance of the injunction, for, by definition, the plaintiff has no (adequate) remedy at law. What is needed to avoid this paradox is not a new verbal formula that subordinates the injunction, but one that ties its availability to the legislative decision about other remedies and thus the existence of the substantive right.

3. State Courts

In the early part of the nineteenth century it was not unusual for there to be one chancellor for an entire state and a system of common law courts widely dispersed throughout that state. In such a setting, the subordination of the injunction furthered

interests in localism. Those institutional arrangements are now
at an end, but, oddly enough, in recent years the irreparable
injury requirement has been made to serve comparable interests, as a means of fixing the bounds between state and federal
courts. The starting point was that extraordinary day in 1943
when the Supreme Court decided both *Murdock* v. *Pennsylvania*[34] and *Douglas* v. *City of Jeannette*.[35]

Both cases involved the same ordinance of the City of Jeannette. The ordinance prohibited solicitation without a license.
The issue was whether the First Amendment allowed the ordinance to be applied to the familiar solicitation activities of
Jehovah's Witnesses. In *Murdock* the Supreme Court reviewed
criminal convictions for violating the ordinance, and in *Douglas*
v. *City of Jeannette* the Court was asked to review the dismissal
of an injunctive suit brought in federal court to restrain the
enforcement of the ordinance.

The Supreme Court first announced its decision in *Murdock:*
the ordinance was unconstitutional as applied to the Jehovah's
Witnesses. Then the Court turned to *Douglas* v. *City of Jeannette*. One might have expected the Court to affirm (or possibly
vacate and remand) on the theory that the *Murdock* declaration of unconstitutionality made an injunction against the
enforcement of the ordinance unnecessary; that disposition
would have implicated the familiar principle requiring the
plaintiff to show the need for the relief—the likelihood of a
future wrong. Obviously, so the Court could have reasoned, its
own contemporaneous decision in *Murdock* radically changed
the picture as it might have existed at the time the *Douglas* suit
was filed or at the time the district court acted; now there was
no reason to assume the ordinance would be enforced against
the *Douglas* v. *City of Jeannette* plaintiffs. This line of reasoning would have kept the case at a low visibility. It is mentioned
in the opinion, but the Court chose to rest its affirmance on a
much more ambitious theory.

The *Douglas* v. *City of Jeannette* theory had two prongs: the first was to claim that a vital principle of federalism was threatened by the injunctive suit, and the second was to use the irreparable injury requirement to eliminate that threat to federalism. The result was to create, in our remedial hierarchy, a preference for the state criminal defense—you must use it if you can. Both this result and its underlying theory, renewed by the "Our Federalism" shibboleth of *Younger* v. *Harris* some thirty years later, strike me as flawed. The injunctive suit posed no threat to federalism correctly perceived, and, even if it did, the irreparable injury requirement is an inadequate means of safeguarding federalist values.

It is hard to believe that the state interest being vindicated by *Douglas* v. *City of Jeannette* is of any moment, is in any sense vital. It was *Murdock* v. *Pennsylvania,* not *Douglas* v. *City of Jeannette,* that made the fundamental points about federal structure: the states are bound by federal law, including the Bill of Rights, and the ultimate power to determine the consistency of the state laws with these superior federal norms is allocated to a federal court, the Supreme Court of the United States. Moreover, given the nature of the claim—that a state is violating the federal Constitution—it is hard to see how the *Douglas* rule could serve the usual values of localism, such as a desire to have law enforcement reflect local community sentiments, which a federal district court is not likely to express. In matters constitutional, nationwide uniformity is a necessity.

At best, *Douglas* v. *City of Jeannette* was a gesture: it might be viewed as a means of safeguarding certain dignitary interests. The preference for the criminal defense could be justified on the theory that state officials should not be gratuitously insulted (as might have occurred if the Supreme Court assumed the City of Jeannette District Attorney was going to enforce the ordinance in the face of the declaration of unconstitutionality). This interpretation is all the more credible in light of the more recent progeny of *Douglas* v. *City of Jeannette,* such as *Younger* v. *Harris* and *Wooley* v. *Maynard*,[36] making the nonpendency of a state prosecution the touchstone—a necessary and almost a sufficient condition—for access to federal injunctive relief. The no-prosecution-pending rule might be seen as intended to avoid the irritation that might be caused if state officials are stopped by a federal district court from going forward with a case that has already been launched. And the primary concern must be with the sensibilities of state prosecutors; they would be the addressees of the *Douglas* type of injunction. It is truly difficult, though not impossible, to imagine a state judge noticing—much less taking offense—when a case ceases to appear on his ever-crowded calendar.

Douglas involved a preventive injunction, one intended to stop the enforcement of a statute on grounds of its unconstitutionality, and it is to those types of injunctions that the rule of that case is primarily addressed. Yet I presume it is applicable to the reparative injunction, and in fact in *Littleton* the theory was used in the structural context .The Court saw in the structural injunction there requested an even greater threat to the values of "Our Federalism," and threw down a bar more impenetrable than the no-prosecution-pending rule. The Court understood that the structural injunction would have placed the federal district court in the position of supervising the conduct of state officials—state judges—over a long period of time, and as a consequence insisted that the injunction be compared to a long and novel list of alternative remedies, presumed the adequacy of these alternative remedies, and required that, in any event, the irreparable injury be "great and immediate."

There is of course a place in the law for a gesture, but the premises that underlie this one seem most doubtful—the amount of insult exaggerated. The insult must be gauged at the margin. In the *Douglas* context the appropriate question is not whether a federal injunction would offend the district attorney, but rather how much more irritation it would cause than, for example, the state court's granting the defendant's motion to dismiss the indictment. This, of course, assumes that the plaintiff has a meritorious claim and that the state court would view it as fairly as would the federal court. If, on the other hand, one assumed the state trial courts would not be equally fair, the remittitur to the state courts would be even more impossible to justify on the insult theory; for the irritation caused by the federal district court injunction would pale once compared to the irritation caused by the scenario in which the state trial court denied a motion to dismiss, there was a trial, a conviction, and then a reversal by a state appellate court or by the United States Supreme Court. Any other scenario would be inconsistent with the very idea of a national constitution.

A similar point could be made if we shifted our focus to other types of injunctions. State officials—in this instance, state judges—would of course be offended by the continuous supervision required by the decree sought in *Littleton,* but the offense would not be much greater than that which would flow from the use of other remedies there given a primacy, federal habeas or criminal prosecutions, constant reversals, or state procedures to remove a judge. Once again, we must keep constant our assumption about the merits of plaintiff's claim, and if so, it is fair to assume that the amount of the *marginal* irritation attributed to the federal injunction is small, hardly of any moment.

These conjectures about marginal irritation are, of course, fraught with error. The irritation might be greater than I have imagined, particularly if the focus in the *Douglas* context shifts, as it had in *Littleton,* to the sensibilities of state judges rather than district attorneys. Maybe it is the very *idea* of a federal court injunction against a pending prosecution that offends. Even so, I should emphasize, the case for the *Douglas* gesture has not yet been made. For there is a price to be paid. The marginal irritation avoided by the *Douglas* rule must be placed alongside the value denied—respect for the claimant's choice of forum.

The post–Civil War jurisdictional revision did not obligate the constitutional claimant to utilize the federal courts. Yet it is equally true that Congress gave him an option (in 28 U.S.C. §§ 1331 and 1343, plus 42 U.S.C. § 1983—the latter being viewed as a jurisdictional trigger). From the pre–Civil War perspective, "Our Federalism" might have meant, "You must use the state courts if you can." But from the post–Civil War perspective, which takes into account the fundamental change brought about by this reconstituting event, "Our Federalism" means, "You can use the federal courts if you choose (even if the assumption of jurisdiction would offend state officials)." The *Douglas* v. *City of Jeannette* gesture honors state officials but at the price of interfering with the exercise of this choice—a result that could be conceptualized in dignitary terms. It shows disrespect for the citizen's judgment about which forum will best adjudicate his grievance against the state.

Of course, the citizen-claimant's decision to utilize the federal district court may be premised on an incorrect assessment of the fairness of the state courts. But there is no *sound* way of second-guessing or reviewing that decision. In order to second-guess the citizen-claimant's choice of the federal forum, the federal court must either (a) engage in irrebuttable presumptions (e.g., the state courts are fair) or (b) place the state courts on trial. The first alternative, the irrebuttable presumption, flies in the face of the little we know from experience, particularly the civil rights experience.[37] The second alternative, a federal court trial on the question of whether the relevant state court is fair, is almost unthinkable. It would make every federal injunctive suit consume enormous resources and overburden the front end of the litigation. Even more importantly, it would defeat the very interest to be served. The federal court inquiry itself would be a massive affront to state officials.

I therefore believe the *Douglas* v. *City of Jeannette* theory of federalism is unsound: the interests protected are exaggerated; it overlooks the countervailing interests; and it results in either unrealistic assumptions or self-defeating inquiries by the federal courts. There is more. Even if this analysis of its theory of federalism is not correct, *Douglas* v. *City of Jeannette* can be faulted on a second ground—the use of the irreparable injury doctrine to demarcate the bounds of the state and federal courts.

This linguistic borrowing is a kind of legal prestidigitation. The Court would have us believe that it is only making a point about remedies, when it is in fact making a point about the structure of the federal system (or, even worse, a point about the sensibilities of state officials). The irreparable injury formula invokes the traditions of equity, and thereby enables the Court to forward its view of federalism without having to justify fully its value preference—safeguarding the sensibilities of the state official at the expense of voiding the citizen claimant's exercise of a congressionally conferred option. The language of equity is a prop for the value preference; full responsibility is thereby avoided.

In addition, the irreparable injury formula is a poor tool for serving the *Douglas* v. *City of Jeannette* preference—it is too narrow a lens. The irreparable injury requirement brings into focus only the (state) noninjunctive remedies, and requires them to be compared to the (federal) injunction. Only the noninjunctive remedies—damages action, criminal prosecution, and, most notably in this context, the criminal defense—are examined for inadequacy. If and only if they are inadequate will the (federal) injunction be available. But if the Court is really committed to "Our Federalism"—to force the constitutional claimant to use the state courts if he can—the comparison ought to be between the federal injunction and *all* state remedies, including the state court injunction.

Another verbal formula—such as "comity"—might cure this defect; that formula might broaden the lens and permit the state injunctive remedy to be considered as an alternative to the federal injunction. But this shift from "irreparable injury" to "comity" would be more than a minor semantic change. The word "comity" would make it clear that what is being subordinated is not a remedy, the injunction, but rather a system of courts. A jurisdictional hierarchy may come to replace the remedial one, and although the jurisdictional hierarchy may also be criticized on the ground I have already suggested—that it rests on an unsound theory of federalism—at the very least the central purpose of this essay will have been achieved—to bring an end to the remedial hierarchy. One hierarchy at a time.

C. THE ARGUMENT FROM LIBERTY

The literature abounds with quaint statements suggesting that the injunction is a disfavored remedy because it entails an excessive restraint on liberty. The injunction is characterized as the "strong arm of the Chancellor"; the noninjunctive remedies are said to be "gentler."[38] This language has a certain charm, but quite frankly I find it difficult to make much sense out of it (or similar arguments focussing on the fusion of power in the injunctive process). The mere fact that the injunction is a restraint on the defendant's liberty—an "effective" restraint, a "powerful" one—cannot count against it; for from one view of the case—the only one we can assume since it is the view adopted by a court after a full adversary hearing—the defendant either is about to or has already engaged in conduct that is both illegal and harmful. The very purpose of the injunction is to stop that conduct or to correct its effects.[39] What must be critical, then, in this argument from liberty is the claim that the restraint is *excessive,* and that claim remains unintelligible without some sense of what is the *right* degree of restraint.

1. Special Liberties: The Prior Restraint Doctrine

The prior restraint doctrine represents one attempt to come to terms with this central quandary of the argument from liberty. This doctrine focusses on one liberty—a liberty that can most readily support an argument for absolute immunity—the liberty to speak. Under this view, the "right" degree of restraint is "no" restraint, or, more modestly, "almost no" restraint.

This subordinating doctrine is flawed by a failure to explain adequately why special disabilities are attached to the injunction alone, why the injunction is disfavored compared to other remedies. If the operative assumption is that the right degree of restraint is "no" restraint, then there should be an equally stringent ban on the noninjunctive remedies. All restraints on speech should be tested by the troop movement paradigm. There are differences between the injunction and the other legal remedies; yet it is not clear why these differences work out in any general or systematic fashion to disfavor the injunction, to require that the injunction be held to a standard—"no restraint"—not applied to other remedies.

The prior restraint doctrine primarily applies to the classic preventive injunction, and as we saw, those injunctions might be deemed preventive in the sense that their issuance is not conditioned on a past wrong. But we also saw that liability rules and criminal prohibitions are in that same sense preventive instruments. The deterrent effect of these legal instruments does not await the appearance of a book or the delivery of a speech; these instruments may induce silence just as effectively as an injunction. On occasion this point has been well understood by the Court; it underlies the overbreadth doctrine,[40] intended to curb the "chilling effect" of criminal statutes. But the similarity between injunctions, liability rules, and criminal prohibitions, that they all have a "chilling effect," seems to be lost when the Court turns to the prior restraint doctrine and holds injunctions to a much more rigorous substantive standard than the other prior restraints.

Nor can the special disability of the injunction be justified in terms of its individuated quality, arguably a distinguishing feature of the injunction. On the contrary, individuation should work to the advantage of the injunction. Individuation is the antithesis of overbreadth; it is a means of containing the "chilling effect" of a prohibition, and from the perspective of the First Amendment, that is supposed to be good.

Similarly, the decentralized character of the injunctive process, the fact that it allocates power of initiation to the citizen, cannot justify the special treatment. Such an argument overlooks the decentralized character of damage actions (including those asking for punitive damages). It also ignores the fact that the true analog of the injunction is not the criminal prosecution but the criminal prohibition. Criminal prohibitions (and liability rules) are operative—"chill"—without the specific invocation of a district attorney. Criminal contempt may be analogous to the criminal prosecution, but it should be noted that the power of initiation in criminal contempt is (at least formally) allocated to the court, an agency more likely to be solicitous of First Amendment rights than a political officer such as the district attorney.

Can the subordination of the injunction in this domain be justified on the theory that it is more *effective?* Harry Kalven once suggested that the prior restraint doctrine might be seen as "protecting the chance for civil disobedience"[41]—a chance to be prized if one believes in the absolutist rule or in human fallibility—that legal agencies, even after a full hearing, can make mistakes. Professor Kalven was responding to the *Pentagon*

Papers case and, more particularly, the highly publicized commitment by the *New York Times* to abide by the outcome of the injunctive proceeding the Attorney General was theatening —a commitment to obey whatever injunction he might obtain—even though the *Times* presumably had been willing to run the risk of a criminal prosecution under the Espionage Act. The *Times* was willing to disobey the criminal statute, but not the injunction.

Professor Kalven's insight is an illuminating account of the *Pentagon Papers* case, and yet it is hard to generalize it into a justification of the prior restraint doctrine and the special disabilities imposed on the injunction as a regulation of speech. The special power of the injunction seems to be confined to the commitment of the *Times.* Such a commitment cannot generally be expected, especially from a citizen who is willing to disobey a criminal statute. Indeed, no one seems to know what prompted the *Times* to make its commitment,[42] and the subsequent repudiation of the commitment by the *Times*[43]—even the *Times,* a paragon of respectability—is revealing.

The argument for greater effectiveness might rest on the view that civil disobedience to an injunction involves a "repudiation" of a very special and highly personalized relationship between the law and the citizen. This might well be true; as I noted in chapter 2, the injunctive process does personalize the law.[44] But there is no reason to suppose that a citizen is not willing to incur these costs—to flout the mystique or violate the special relationship—or is less willing to incur them than the analogous costs involved in disobeying a statute. It all depends. . . . The civil rights experience may have enhanced the tranquilizing power of the (federal) courts; on the other hand, the labor experience, both past and present, teaches us that the injunction could have precisely the opposite effect, enhancing the moral imperative of disobedience.

The argument for greater effectiveness is no more successful if we turn from these more subtle ways of explaining the sway of the injunction—the mystique theory—and instead assume a rational calculator model, where behavior is predicted on the basis of the likely effect of sanction. There is no reason to assume, as a general systematic proposition, that the sanction for disobeying an injunction is more effective in coercing compliance—effectively foreclosing the option of civil disobedience—than the sanction of a criminal prohibition, for instance.

I have my doubts whether disobedience of an injunction will be detected and prosecuted more vigorously than disobedience of a criminal statute, given the very special kind of conduct we are envisioning—speech that purports to be a form of civil disobedience. More often than not, the decision of civil disobedience is made in the face of a threat to prosecute if the citizen engages in the proposed conduct or does not abandon the course of conduct he is now pursuing. Such a threat might indeed be essential to the dynamics of civil disobedience (and, as the Justices knew, was in fact present in the *Pentagon Papers* case—by the time they decided the case Attorney General Mitchell was threatening criminal prosecutions under the subversion statutes[45]). From the ante hoc perspective, the injunction might be seen as the functional equivalent of such a threat.

But even if I am wrong on this score, even if there is no such threat, or alternatively the citizen believes that disobedience of an injunction will be a more certain trigger of a valid prosecutorial response, that would only affect the likelihood of imposition of the sanctions, the certainty factor. The severity factor must also be considered, for the deterrent effect of a sanction equals the likelihood of imposition times the severity of the expected sanction. The certainty factor is likely to be higher with injunctions, and yet the severity factor is characteristically much lower.[46] This is particularly true if the judge wishes to avoid a jury and capture the benefit of his *concentration* of power, for he must then confine himself to petty punishments.

This point is not altered by the rule of *Walker* v. *City of Birmingham*—a rule that, I note in passing, seems at odds with the prior restraint doctrine, for it purports to give the injunction a power withheld from criminal statutes, even in the speech domain. This rule affects only the likelihood of imposition. The citizen is precluded from raising a defense in the enforcement proceeding. But he is still free to disobey the injunction and suffer the consequences, which are likely to be more petty than those attached to criminal statutes. The penalty in the *Walker* case was five days in jail and a fifty-dollar fine—the maximum permitted by state statute.

Conditional-order civil contempt has a greater chance of precluding civil disobedience: conceivably, the individual can be imprisoned until the judge is absolutely assured of compliance. Initially, it should be noted that this sanction is only available after one act of civil disobedience, and thus is comparable to the specific deterrent effect of a damage action[47] or a criminal prosecution. (These remedies require a past wrong, but have an effect on the future conduct of the defendant and the citizenry in general.) Moreover, if conditional-order civil contempt were the principal sanction feared, the *first* act of civil disobedience would be much more likely (for no punishment would attach to that act). True, the second act of civil disobedience may be more unlikely because the judge need not engage in speculative probabilistic judgments, as in the criminal system, about how severely the citizen must be punished today to discourage him from doing it again tomorrow. Yet, from another view, speech might be thought to be the winner because conditional-order civil contempt—a highly calibrated instrument of specific deterrence—is less likely to have as broad a "chilling effect" as a damage award or criminal conviction. The calibrated quality of conditional-order civil contempt may be a boon to speech.

Finally, one should not think of the injunction as foreclosing the opportunity for civil disobedience and thus posing a special danger to speech on the theory that it—and it alone—is the trigger of incapacitation. The *Debs* case naturally leads one to think of incapacitation. Federal troops were used in the Pullman Strike as an adjunct to the injunction, and Eugene Debs claimed in the course of the inquiry by the federal commission that what truly broke the Pullman Strike was his arrest and imprisonment in the course of the strike—incapacitation that precluded him from issuing directives (speaking) to the strikers.[48] But what we must remember is that although the injunction may be a sufficient condition for incapacitation, it is not a necessary condition. Incapacitation is not a sanction confined to the injunction; arrests (of speakers) and seizures (of books) are as integral a part of the criminal process as they are of the injunctive process. Debs could have been arrested and presumably the troops used even without an injunction. Indeed, since the injunctive process implicates a court rather than just the local district attorney and arresting officers, the principal operatives of the pretrial level of the criminal process, incapacitation in the injunctive context is likely to be kept at a highly visible level and thus used more responsibly. It is likely to pose less of a threat to free speech.

2. General Liberties: Compensation and the Optimum Degree of Restraint

I have suggested that the preventive injunction might profitably be compared to a criminal prohibition. This perspective exposes the fallacy of the prior restraint doctrine. At the same time it might be thought to create a new argument for subordination, one that would not be confined to the liberty to speak but would reach all liberties in an undifferentiated manner. This view of an injunction as a mini-criminal statute brings into focus the recent critique of the criminal law by welfare economists who can be read as proposing, as a normative matter, that criminal prohibitions be supplanted by liability rules.[49] The criminal law should become a branch of torts. Their core idea, so reminiscent of Holmes's positivism,[50] is that a restraint on liberty greater than that entailed in threatening to internalize the costs of an individual's action is "excessive." They argue that individuals should be free to do whatever they want provided they are made to pay the full costs of their action.

The injunctive sanctioning system as it presently exists includes the possibility of punishment, and since, as I have argued, sanctioning systems must be judged by the whole range of sanctions, including the most severe, it is vulnerable to this economic critique. This criticism could be muffled by a revision in the injunctive system. If we were convinced that the sanction should be exclusively compensatory, then compensatory-damage civil contempt could be made the exclusive sanction for violation of an injunction. This revision would not render the injunction superfluous, reducing it to a liability rule by another name. For the injunction has an individuated quality not possessed by liability rules and a different allocation of the power to decide, attributes of considerable utility.

To be certain, I do not recommend the revision. I am not persuaded by the economic critique. I reject the reductionism of right to remedy implicit in this critique and in Holmes's positivism. My conceptual world has been shaped in large part by the civil rights experience, and at the core of that experience is a conception of rights that denies their reducibility to a series of propositions assuring the payment of money to the victims. I acknowledge the interdependence of remedy and right (in, for example, my discussion on the unrealistic quality of bifurcated procedures[51]), but this presupposes rather than denies the distinction between the two.

As a purely analytic matter this reductionism can be faulted on the ground that it does not give an adequate account of

ordinary language. It blurs, for example, the distinction between *justifying* the imposition of a sanction (e.g., damages),
and *predicting* it.[52] But the response has to be more substantive,
for the economic critique has a normative dimension. It seeks
to reform our practices and, if need be, our language.

The substantive response derives, first, from a concern with
the distributional consequences of a purely compensatory regime. The liberty of the judgment-proof would be enhanced.
So would the liberty of the very wealthy, assuming declining
marginal utility of each dollar and an incapacity to introduce
a principle of progressivity into the damage award, most plausible assumptions.

Second, I am troubled by the impossibility of placing a mone-
tary value on all injuries, either those to individual victims (the
loss of the view of the oak) or the public generally (a deteriora-
tion of an aesthetic quality of the community.)[53]

Third, there is the impossibility of adequately compensating
for fear. Initially there is the fear of a violation. One could
respond by including that fear as an element of compensation—
if you are a victim you will be compensated for injuries, including the fear of ever becoming a victim. But that assurance does
not allay the fear of becoming a victim, for that fear is linked
to a second fear, namely, the fear that you will not be fully
compensated (despite all these assurances). And once you try
to take care of that second-order fear through another assurance
of compensation for even that second-order fear, you are led
back to an infinite regression, always leaving a residue of
uncompensated fear.[54]

Finally, I question the central premise of the economic
critique—that a compensatory regime will improve allocative
efficiency, which in turn will maximize total social product. The
economist starts with the insight that the perpetrator will engage
in "prohibited" action if and only if the proposed course of
conduct is worth more to him than the amount of the victim's

damages he has to pay. Under an exclusively compensatory regime the victim would receive full compensation, the perpetrator would be left with a net benefit (the difference between the compensation bill and the benefit to him), and total social value would thereby be maximized. On the other hand, so the argument continues, under a prohibitory regime, where the sanction is greater than the damage to the victim, the perpetrator may be stopped from pursuing the more valuable course of conduct. There would be a failure to maximize total value and thus an excessive restraint on liberty. The central fallacy with this argument is that it ignores the bargaining process.[55]

Let us assume an ordinary trespass case, where the plaintiff seeks an injunction to stop the defendant from taking some goods from his land. Let us also assume that this is a case in which the goods do not have a sentimental value (not the silver chalice), but are entirely of a commercial nature (rocks used for construction). This would be a case in which the court would surely invoke the irreparable injury requirement, remitting the plaintiff to the damage remedy, and yet it is hard to understand the economic logic of such a result.

The injunction would not stop the defendant from obtaining the goods. It would merely force him to negotiate with the plaintiff before taking his goods. The injunction only requires that the defendant purchase the owner's consent. The plaintiff and defendant must bargain, and as long as this is done before the decree is violated, I can perceive of no reason why that bargain would not be given effect. The very decentralized character of initiation in the injunctive process facilitates the bargaining: the would-be victim commenced the suit and presumably can have the decree vacated and the suit dismissed.

There remains a question about what price will be charged— can it be presumed that, in terms of allocative efficiency, the damage award would be superior to the price likely to result from the injunctive bargaining? I think not.

Let us first consider a competitive situation—many buyers and many sellers. Then the price the plaintiff can insist upon in the injunctive bargaining will be limited by the price being charged by other sellers: if it is higher the defendant will "obey" the injunction, that is, purchase the goods from a seller other than the plaintiff. Accordingly, in a competitive situation the injunctive bargaining is likely to result in the market price. Damages should also reflect the market price, which in a competitive situation is equal to what the plaintiff would charge the defendant. Thus it might even be said that in terms of efficiency, the injunction is the superior remedy—it should be given a primacy—for the injunction avoids the dangers and costs inherent in having a third party guess what two others might agree upon. At best, the damage award mirrors what the outcome of the injunctive negotiations would be; it merely remits the decision to a third party, such as the jury.

Ironically, in the competitive situation the preference for the damage remedy creates the very incentive for the defendant to commit the trespass. The defendant may be counting on a runaway jury—he may be assuming an especially sympathetic adjudicator that would be present in the damage action but not in a contempt proceeding, one that is likely to set the damage award lower than the negotiated price, either in the market or within the framework of the injunction. This strategy is an intelligible one, but there is no economic reason why it should be honored; indeed there is every reason why it should be discouraged.

The competitive assumption does not exhaust the world. There are monopoly situations, but even then the reason for preferring damages is not clear to me. In the case of the bilateral monopoly, a single seller and a single buyer,[56] the injunction is still preferable. It forces the parties to set the price by bargaining and thus avoids the awkwardness of calling on a third party to set a price that in truth is indeterminate. In a bilateral monopoly, there is no economic "right" price, in any objective sense, but rather an indifference to whatever happens to be the outcome of the bargaining (assuming there are no imperfections in that process).

In a unilateral monopoly, the case of a single seller and many buyers, the damage remedy might produce a result more consonant with the dictates of efficiency because damages could be set at marginal cost, which is lower than what the monopolist would charge. On the other hand, this strikes me as a perverse way of regulating a monopolist—rewarding those buyers adventurous enough to steal from the monopolist—and might even be counterproductive, for over time the loss of revenue might induce the monopolist to restrict production further. The issue as to what should be the measure of damages for a monopolist needs further exploration, but in any event, even if the measure of damages should be lower than what the monopolist would ask within the framework of the injunctive bargaining process, the justification for the irreparable injury requirement in its present guise—as a general requirement—is still wanting. At best, we have located a justification for its applicability to a unilateral monopolist.

Whether we are faced with a competitive or monopoly situation, the bargaining process may break down because of, for example, strategic behavior (e.g., the bluff that does not work) or information barriers. There are two points to be made. First, there are comparable dangers of failure in the damage action; there is no general, systematic reason for believing that the damages are more immune to such problems. This is true even of the multiparty situation, where bargaining is commonly thought to be especially frail and costly. The injunction creates the possibility of having the judge supervise or at least facilitate the bargaining, and there is no reason for believing that such a process is more costly or more prone to failure than the omnibus damage action. Second, even if the damage action is assumed to provide some comparative advantage in this setting, there is no reason to believe that this setting is the typical one. Indeed, I suspect that it is the exception, and if so my central point remains: the subordination of the injunction, as a general, systematic proposition, cannot be justified on the theory that the injunction is excessively coercive. The excess above compensation produces negotiation and bargaining, not allocative inefficiency.

D. THE ARGUMENT FROM THE DIFFICULTY OF PROPHESYING

Insofar as the injunction seeks to prevent a future wrong, it requires the court to make predictions about the future, and these judgments are widely assumed to be treacherous, fraught with error. The question raised is whether the burden of prophecy justifies the subordination of the injunction.

I believe this argument fails, first, because it lacks generality. Informational difficulty might justify the subordination of the preventive injunction, but certainly not the reparative injunction, and maybe even not the structural injunction. These latter two injunctions have informational problems of their own, but those difficulties flow from the nature of the enterprise, not the remedy. They are independent of the remedy. Consider, for example, the informational problems inherent in a program of black reparations, or the ones that might arise in an attempt to deal with school segregation through damage awards.

Second, the argument does not sufficiently reflect the predictive elements embedded in alternative legal instruments. Here I have in mind, for example, the criminal statute, which basically resembles the preventive injunction. The injunction is distinguished from the criminal statute in that it is individuated and promulgated by a judge, and the power of initiation is decentralized. But none of these characteristics intensifies the burden of prophesying. It is hard to believe that the legislature has unique informational resources, ones that would enhance the accuracy of judgments about the future. Similarly, I do not understand why individuation enhances error. On the contrary, the generality of the criminal prohibition only compounds risks of error. Individuation permits a certain modesty.

Finally, the argument exaggerates both the need to prophesy, the risk of error, and the costs of a mistaken prophecy. The preventive injunction seeks to prevent a future wrong, and it is customarily conditioned upon a showing that there is a probability (of some indeterminate magnitude) of that future wrong's occurring.[57] The element of prophecy goes to the *need* for the remedy. I doubt that this judgment of need is more treacherous than many of the judgments implied in alternative remedies, such as those involving questions of motivation or causation, which might be present in injunctive proceedings but which take an increased urgency and stringency in remedies such as damage actions and criminal prosecutions.[58] Those remedies call for the reconstruction of an historical event, where the decisional agency did not "experience" that event but rather comes to understand it only through the narratives of persons whose social situation, if not their perspective, is likely to have been determined by that event. The risk of error is notorious— no less so, I imagine, than that introduced by the need to prophesy. In any event, I wonder whether the costs of a mistaken prophecy have been exaggerated.

Assume the judge denies the injunction when in truth there is a need for it. The plaintiff is left without protection of the injunction. But surely he is no worse off than under a regime of subordination, where he would have to rely exclusively on the deterrent effect of liability rules and criminal prohibitions. Alternatively, assume the judge issues the injunction when in truth there is no need for it. Then the defendant is restrained, but only from engaging in conduct that a court has determined is illegal and injurious to plaintiff. The mistaken prophecy results in an unnecessary exertion of judicial power, not an incorrect one. Some have argued that judicial power should be viewed as a wasting asset, and thus an unnecessary exertion of judicial power may be a special source of concern; but in the battle of metaphors, it is equally plausible to view the judicial power as a muscle, strengthened from use, atrophied from nonuse.

At times more may be at stake than just an unnecessary exertion of judicial power: the judge may be wrong not just about the need for relief, but also about the substantive issues—the rights and duties of the parties. But, subject to two exceptions, the risk of a substantive error is not enhanced by the prophesying element, i.e., that the issuance of the injunction is predicated on a judgment of future need. The risk of substantive error is independent of the informational difficulties of making statements about the future.

One exception arises from *Walker* v. *City of Birmingham.* That case legitimated a state rule precluding the defendant from challenging the constitutional validity of an injunction (to be more precise, a temporary restraining order) in a criminal contempt proceeding. This rule enhances the risk of substantive error by curtailing the self-corrective processes of the law and limiting the incentives a trial judge has to be right. And the *Walker* rule might be thought to be linked to the forward-looking element of the injunction. The rule might be seen as an attempt to perfect the preventive power of the interlocutory injunction, conceived of as a means of freezing the status quo for a period long enough to permit the full adjudication of plaintiff's claim.

This connection between the prospective or preventive element of the injunction and the heightened risk of substantive error is not a logical one: it is more in the nature of an explanatory connection. This is important for it means that the two can be severed. The interlocutory injunction can still serve its preventive function—preserve the status quo—without the *Walker* rule. *Walker* may be overruled, a most salutary result in my judgment since it is inconsistent with the conception of law that subordinates governmental officials—judges—to the Constitution (for it allows an individual to be punished for disobeying a constitutionally invalid judicial command). Or more modestly, hints in the opinion of limitations on the rule could be taken more seriously.[59] If additional deterrent strength is needed for preservation of the status quo, a need I am not convinced of, then it could come in the form of increased severity of sanction. That would have the beneficial result of eliminating a rule that permitted an individual to be punished for disobeying a command that is arguably invalid. It would also reduce the risk of substantive error. The trial judge would have to face the contingency of having his decree declared invalid by an appellate court.

A second exception can arise because the substantive judgment might require a judgment about a state of the world not yet in being. In that instance the burden of prophecy is not confined to a judgment about the likelihood that the defendant will engage in certain conduct. It also extends to a judgment about whether the defendant's conduct will be illegal when done.

This problem appears in the speech area (and indeed might be thought of as another justification for the prior restraint doctrine). We attach a special significance to substantive error in that area, and thus it might be profitable to explore the problem through a speech example. Let us assume that the defendant is to make a street corner speech, and the authorities are concerned that the speaker will incite the audience to violence. Under the *Brandenburg* test, the permissibility of stopping speech will turn on two elements—the content of the speech (the *Masses* legacy—are these words of incitement, urging violence as a concrete and immediate course of action) and the likelihood of success (the clear and present danger legacy—will it trigger the violence).[60] Both elements turn on an inquiry into what will transpire on that street corner—the size of the crowd, its mood, the words uttered. And yet if the authorities sought to restrain the speaker by an injunction, the court would be called on to prophesy on these matters. The risk of substantive error would be greatly enhanced.

The root problem here is, of course, the substantive legal standard, *Brandenburg.* I, for one, would not suggest that the substantive standard be abandoned, although that remains an alternative. But once it is understood that the root problem is a substantive one, then we can see that this line of reasoning cannot support a subordinating doctrine such as irreparable injury or prior restraint. These doctrines are at once too broad and too narrow.

These doctrines are too broad in that they purport to apply to all claims, or in the case of prior restraint to all speech claims, and yet the special risk of error we have located is linked to a special type of substantive standard, one that largely requires judgments as to what will transpire in the future. It cannot even be said that all speech claims utilize such a substantive standard (e.g., a claim against an allegedly obscene book or one founded on a copyright).

At the same time, the subordinating doctrines are too narrow, for they place a unique set of restraints on the injunction, whereas the special risk of error is not confined to the injunction. It is present with any preventive instrument governed by this special type of substantive standard. The restraints now placed on the injunction should not be confined to that instrument, but rather should apply with equal force to any legal instrument or remedy that seeks to interfere with the street-corner speaker before the speech takes place—the criminal prohibition or, more particularized manifestations of those laws, prosecutions for conspiracy or for an attempt to incite violence.[61] In sum, although the risk of substantive error may be enhanced by the confluence of the substantive standard and the preventive aspect of the injunction, the appropriate response is not to subordinate the injunction alone, but rather to disfavor all those legal instruments that might be deemed preventive.

IV

The Legacy: New Perspectives on the
Relationship between Rights and Remedies

In attacking the traditional remedial hierarchy I have placed great reliance on what may now be called the context-dependency proposition—the view that reasons for disfavoring the injunction cannot be generalized across the legal system— they do not hold for all types of claims and all types of factual patterns. I point to this proposition now, and abstract it from the previous argument, because it has an important bearing on our understanding of the civil rights experience. The civil rights injunction evidences the truth of that proposition, but then the proposition turns and limits the legacy of that paradigm.

The context-dependency proposition is antithetical to a hierarchical conception of remedies, *any hierarchy*. I used it to evaluate the arguments on behalf of the traditional hierarchy, the one that subordinated the injunction, but it would be equally available against one that sought to give a primacy to the injunction. I doubt that the reasons for preferring the injunction could be generalized across the legal system, any more than those disfavoring it could. Accordingly, although civil rights litigation gave the injunction a primacy, that practice should be viewed as a source of understanding—a basis for questioning the traditional doctrine, one that demanded a different role for the injunction—not a model that should be imposed on the rest of the legal system. The injunction became the primary remedy in civil rights litigation for a very special set of reasons, and it remains to be seen whether those reasons are generalizable.

One set of reasons is technocratic—civil rights litigation presented the courts with technical tasks that could not be performed by remedies other than the injunction, or that could not be performed as well. The conversion of the dual school systems to unitary school systems is a prime example. From a purely technocratic perspective the injunction seemed ideally suited. In contrast to damage judgments or criminal prosecutions, the injunction could more easily accommodate the group nature of the claim, it could provide the requisite specificity and continuing supervision over long periods of time, and it introduced a desired degree of softness—it had a prospective quality, and directives could easily be modified as the courts enhanced their understanding of the constitutional goal and how that goal might be achieved. All this seemed essential for structural reformation.

Similarly, when the demand was to compensate for the systematic and thorough wrongs of slavery, the Jim Crow era, or the more subtle, and recent, forms of discrimination, cash payments seemed peculiarly inadequate. The inadequacy stemmed from considerations much deeper than difficulties of measurement, for these same difficulties inhere in the reparative injunction—in identifying the victims and perpetrators of the past wrong and knowing what conduct (e.g., preferences?) would constitute adequate compensation. The inadequacy stemmed from the group nature of the underlying claim and a belief that only in-kind benefits would effect a change in the *status* of the group.

The injunction was also well suited for the preventive needs of civil rights litigation. To a large extent this litigation was aimed at government officials, and it was fair to presume that they are not as sensitive to the prospect of damage judgments as the businessman working within a competitive framework.

Moreover, in contrast to both damage judgments and criminal prosecutions, the injunction is capable of speaking only to the future, and with great specificity. It thus facilitates a declaration of rights that is only to have prospective effect, a result that seemed entirely appropriate when, as was true of most of the civil rights era, the standards of behavior were being altered radically. Declaratory judgments could also meet these needs, and, in fact, since the late 1960s—largely to avoid restrictions on the injunction such as 28 U.S.C. § 2283 and its doctrinal counterparts—we have seen a tendency to use the declaratory judgment as a substitute for the injunction to establish prospective rules of conduct. But in the 1950s and early 1960s the declaratory judgment was largely undeveloped: the typical civil rights prayer seeking preventive relief, say, against an allegedly invalid statute sought both injunctive and declaratory relief, with no attention to the distinction between the two.

The second reason for the primacy of the injunction in civil rights litigation is more normative. It turns not so much on the content of the injunction and the technical advantages it brings as on the allocation of power implicit in the injunctive process. The injunctive process essentially allocates power to the citizen-grievant (the power of initiation) and to the judiciary (the power of decision). Such an allocation of power was favored because it seemed essential to the success of the civil rights claim.

At issue in the first decade of the civil rights era, from 1954 to 1964, was the reform of governmental practices and structures, primarily those of the Southern states. It was imperative, if that reformist enterprise was to succeed, that aggrieved citizens have the power of initiation. Their efforts could be supplemented by reform litigation brought by other governmental units, such as the federal government, but it could only be a supplement; the individual grievant had to have the power of initiation, to prod, activate, and at times bypass the Attorney

General. For the second decade of the civil rights era, 1964 to 1974, the reformist enterprise became more universal—embracing all governments, North and South, state and federal. It also included private powers—corporations, unions, and universities. This did not lessen the need for the decentralized allocation of the power of initiation; on the contrary, the universalism broadened the coalition of those opposed to the reform and thus threatened the independence of the Executive. The government official, whether he be the elected district attorney or the Attorney General, appointed by and responsible to the President, is ultimately responsive to the pressure this coalition is able to generate, and thus, from the perspective of the reformers, cannot be trusted as the exclusive repository of the power of initiation.

The allocation of power of initiation to the individual citizen needs no strenuous justification; it readily accords with the American traditions of individualism (in the antigovernmental sense). But the allocation of the power of decision to the judiciary requires a very special justification—it is at odds with our democratic traditions. This justification was lacking with the labor injunction; the same was true with the anti-Progressivism injunction, and in that instance the antidemocratic objection was strengthened by a claim that the decisional agency (the judges) lacked "scientific expertise." In the case of the civil rights injunction, however, this special justification for the allocation to the judiciary could be found in the doctrine of "minority rights." Those who sought the help of the injunction to prevent the organization of labor or to nullify Progressive legislation complained of the excesses of democracy and the tyranny of the masses; industrialists mouthed a doctrine of "minority rights." But the blacks were able to give that doctrine a different and truer meaning. They were able to point to certain factors—not just their number, but also their insularity and economic weakness—that deprived the elective process of its presumption of legitimacy and transferred that legitimacy from the legislature (or other representative bodies) to the judiciary. It was not reasonable to expect the judges to be heroes, but the truth of the matter is that many lived up to these unreasonable expectations—they fought the popular pressures at great personal sacrifice and discomfort. The average judge turned out to be more heroic than the average legislator (or juror). And it was just this hope that led civil rights litigators to cast their suits in injunctive form.

To identify these technocratic and normative elements that account for the primacy of the injunction in civil rights litigation is not to deny that there are other areas in which the injunction may achieve a primacy. Other litigative programs may involve comparable needs. Indeed, in several recent cases, somewhat removed from civil rights, classically defined in terms of protecting the racial minority, doctrine has been created that seems to give a primacy to the injunction. In *Pierson* v. *Ray*[1] the Court created an immunity for judicial officers that might be applicable only to damage remedies; in *Edelman* v. *Jordan*,[2] involving the invalidity of a state practice denying welfare payments, the Court cast an Eleventh Amendment immunity around damage actions that is not applicable to injunctive remedies; and when the Court finally—after the long post–*Bell* v. *Hood* interlude—held that constitutional prohibitions of their own force gave rise to actions for damages if they were violated,[3] it also imposed on such damage actions restrictions— such as a good faith defense—not applicable to injunctions. In all these instances we can readily imagine factors comparable to those in the civil rights area that lead to a preference for the injunction.

Context-dependency, then, does not preclude extending the lessons of the civil rights injunction, but it does preclude the kind of generalization that would be necessary to create a new hierarchy. The essential lesson of the civil rights injunction is

not that we should supplant one remedial hierarchy with another, one that would give the injunction a new presumptive
status as the primary remedy; that would only mirror the
Frankfurter and Greene error. Rather, the civil rights injunction
teaches that we should move to a nonhierarchical conception
of remedies. It teaches that the choice of remedy should not
turn on generalized propositions—couched in the obscure but
colorful language of history—about which remedies are favored
and which are disfavored. It should instead turn upon an ap-
preciation of the technical advantages of each remedy and a
judgment, made in light of the substantive claim, about the
desirability of the allocation of power that is implicit in each
remedial system. The civil rights experience teaches that the
rules governing the choice of remedy—procedural rules, if you
will—cannot and should not be fashioned apart from and independent of one's belief about the nature and justice of the
underlying claim. This conception challenges the familiar tenet
of the law demanding that procedure be independent of substance.

Once we move away from a hierarchical conception of remedies, we can also see that the choice before a court is not simply
which remedy, but whether there be *any* remedy, even assuming
a substantive right was violated. The injunction may be the
only remedy available, or it may be vastly superior to any
other, and yet there may be good reasons not to grant it. This
judgment—of a right without a remedy—hardly seemed plausible when the remedy imagined was of modest proportions—a
damage judgment, or a preventive injunction aimed at some
discrete act. The slogan of no-right-without-a-remedy seemed
tautological. But not so once the perspective broadens, as the
civil rights experience dictates that it must, and we consider
the new legal instruments it has spawned, above all the structural injunction.

In thinking about the structural injunction within the hier-

archical context, little could be said against it: the difficulties
with it seemed endemic to the enterprise, and thus were likely
to be as present with the injunction as with other remedies
(whether it be a damage judgment, or even an administrative
scheme).[4] Indeed, as Homer Clark suggested in a review of
my casebook,[5] the special irony of the irreparable injury requirement is that it seems to provide no restraint when restraint
is most needed: the most problematic use of the injunctive
power is in the structural context, and yet that is the instance
in which the alternative remedies are strikingly inadequate. The
point is not simply that the irreparable injury requirement is
inadequate for the task, Clark's insight, but also that it distorts
our perspective on the structural injunction. The irreparable
injury requirement introduces a relativistic or comparative perspective, and in a sense that makes the structural injunction
seem less extraordinary than it is.

The structural injunction is not "extraordinary" in the way
that word has traditionally been used, when the standard of
comparison is other judicial remedies engaged in a similar
enterprise. What is extraordinary about the structural injunction is the nature of the enterprise and what that does to the
judicial office. The structural injunction is extraordinary if the
standard is law, not other remedies. For, as I explained earlier,[6]
the structural injunction should not be conceived of as a discrete
coercive act, like a command backed by a sanction, but rather
as the initiation of a relationship between the judge and an institution—a declaration that the judge will henceforth manage
the reconstruction of an ongoing social institution.

The structural injunction entails a relationship of long duration between the judge and the social institution, a series of
interventions, either increasing the specificity or modifying
previously issued decrees, inviting or permitting participation
by amici, such as the Department of Justice, or possibly even
creating new agencies to assist in the policing of performance.

An auxiliary bureaucratic structure is often created. In economic terms this behavioral pattern is costly. Of even greater concern is its impact on judicial role. The structural injunction tends to accentuate the personification inherent in the injunctive process and to make it difficult for the judge to maintain the umpireal posture. The judge is brought perilously close, so it is claimed, to breaching the line between administration and law.[7]

These considerations—the consumption of resources and even more, the role transformation—render plausible the possibility of a right without a remedy—that the court will decline to issue a structural injunction even though that is by far the best remedy, or for that matter the only remedy. Indeed, that is precisely what the Court did in *Littleton* and more recently in *Rizzo* v. *Goode*[8] (though in *Littleton* it pretended that there were alternative remedies, and in both the result was rationalized in terms of the transjurisdiction point—the plaintiffs were asking a *federal* court to reconstruct the judiciary of Cairo, Illinois, or the Philadelphia police department).

I acknowledge these concerns, and yet I do not concede their persuasiveness. I do not believe the structural injunction should be put beyond the reach of the courts. First of all, while the role transformation inherent in a structural injunction is undeniable, the significance of that role transformation is less clear. Fidelity to role is not a good in and of itself, particularly if, as in this instance, the role does not have any a priori moral basis but rather is largely defined by tradition. A glance at the Continental criminal system reveals the plausibility of a procedural system that abandoned the contest-umpire model; the inquisitorial judge can make errors and abuse his office, but there is no reason to believe that he is more prone in this direction than his passive, umpireal counterpart.[9] Nor should personification be a source of concern. It only demythologizes or demystifies the law. It brings us closer to the truth. The bearer of legal power is a person. Of course, once we concede that, we then have to cope with the limitations that inhere in personhood, and ask ourselves the questions of legitimacy afresh—why should we have to obey this person? But that strikes me as only the beginning of understanding—the question that should indeed be asked.

Second, even if the role transformations inherent in the structural decree are considered a cost and are aggregated with the economic ones, they do not become insurmountable: they only call for more urgent justification. Extraordinary injunctions may require extraordinary claims. What gives legal claims such a special status, the entitlement to be considered "extraordinary," is the special nature of the substantive claim—the systematic denial of important rights to a social group. Thus the departures from the standard models of judicial behavior are ultimately justified and determined by underlying substantive rights. Just as the civil rights experience has undermined the notion that a single rule—such as the irreparable injury requirement—should govern the choice of remedy for all substantive claims, so also has it illustrated the need for unusual, structural remedies when justice so requires. Once again, procedure is not independent of substance. In the context of injunctive remedies, and perhaps other contexts as well, the civil rights era teaches that procedure is, and should be, ineluctably tied to the merits and nature of the underlying substantive claim.

The civil rights claim must be, for us today, a source of perspective, an example but not a fixed rule. It suggests, but should neither automatically legitimate nor delimit, the usefulness of structural relief. The formal classification of a legal claim—the fact that it can be viewed as a civil rights claim advanced on behalf of a racial minority—does not automatically render it extraordinary. Instead, we must employ a more complex form of analysis, one that takes into consideration such factors as the importance of the claim for the eradication of caste structure and the magnitude of the social dislocation that would be caused by honoring the claim.[10] At the same time, it should be recognized that a claim need not be a civil rights one in order to be deemed extraordinary; many of the claims concerning prisons, mental institutions, and the environment may have that quality. The lesson of the civil rights injunction can be broadened by analogy.

In searching for the limits of the lesson of the civil rights experience we should also understand that a claim need not have moral force before it is considered extraordinary, sufficient to justify the costs of a structural injunction. I do not mean to deny the moral status of the civil rights claim, but only to recognize the power of the law. The moral status of a claim may derive from its legal recognition: morality shaped the judgment in *Brown* v. *Board of Education,* and that judgment then shaped our morality. Shrouded in the mantle of the Constitution, dedicated to the reasoned elaboration of our communal ideals, courts have a unique capacity to create the terms of their own legitimacy.

Notes

I. The Triumph of *Brown*

1. 158 U.S. 564 (1895).
2. 198 U.S. 45 (1905).
3. 209 U.S. 123 (1908). The principal precedent upon which the Court built, Reagan v. Farmers' Loan and Trust Co., 154 U.S. 362 (1894), was decided roughly at the same time as *Debs* and written by the same Justice, David Brewer. *Cf. also* Smyth v. Ames, 169 U.S. 466, *modified*, 171 U.S. 361 (1898), in which Brewer served as the trial judge.
4. Act of June 18, 1910, ch. 309, § 17, 36 Stat. 539 (current version at 28 U.S.C. § 2281 (1970)) repealed by Pub. L. 94–381, § 1, Aug. 12, 1976, 90 Stat. 1119. Section 7 of the Evarts Act of 1891, ch. 517, § 7, 26 Stat. 826 (current version at 28 U.S.C. § 1292(a) (1970)), making an order granting an interlocutory injunction appealable notwithstanding a final decision rule, might be understood in a similar fashion.
5. Ch. 323, §§ 15, 17, 19, 21, 22, 38 Stat. 730. The current version of § 15 (limitation on temporary restraining orders) is codified at 15 U.S.C. § 25 (1970); §§ 17 and 19 (effect of injunctions) have been incorporated into FED. R. CIV. P. 65; §§ 21 and 22 (jury trial) are currently codified at 18 U.S.C. § 3691 (1970).
6. Act of Oct. 15, 1914, ch. 323, § 20, 38 Stat. 730 (current version at 29 U.S.C. § 52 (1970)).
7. Act of March 23, 1932, ch. 90, 47 Stat. 70 (codified at 29 U.S.C. §§ 101–115 (1970)).
8. 347 U.S. 483 (1954); 349 U.S. 294 (1955).
9. Wyatt v. Stickney, 344 F. Supp. 373 (M.D. Ala. 1972), *aff'd in part and rev'd in part sub nom.* Wyatt v. Aderholt, 503 F.2d 1305 (5th Cir. 1974) (mental hospital); and Pugh v. Locke, 406 F. Supp. 318 (M.D. Ala. 1976), *aff'd in part and rev'd in part sub nom.* Newman v. Alabama, 559 F.2d 283 (5th Cir. 1977) (prison case). On these cases,

see Note, *The* Wyatt *Case: Implementation of a Judicial Decree Ordering Institutional Change*, 84 YALE L.J. 1338 (1975); Robbins & Buser, *Punitive Conditions of Prison Confinement: An Analysis of* Pugh v. Locke *and Federal Court Supervision of State Penal Administration Under the Eighth Amendment*, 29 STAN. L. REV. 893 (1977).

10. Also, because of the collapse of the common law writs and a failure to exploit the full potential of the new declaratory judgment provisions, the injunction became the primary means for obtaining the more standard form of judicial review of administrative action. This development also increased the prominence of the injunction, for during the 1950s and 1960s judicial review of administrative action became more common.

II.   The Sources of Uniqueness

1. 2 J. STORY, COMMENTARIES ON EQUITY JURISPRUDENCE 154–55 (2d ed., Boston, 1839).

2. *See, e.g.*, S. DAGGETT, RAILROAD REORGANIZATION (1908); E. DODD & D. BILLYOU, CASES AND MATERIALS ON CORPORATE REORGANIZATIONS 1–24 (1950); W. MOORE, THE REORGANIZATION OF RAILROAD CORPORATIONS 1–16 (1941).

3. *See, e.g.*, United States v. E. I. Du Pont De Nemours & Co., 366 U.S. 316, 326–35 (1961).

4. *See* the cases and authorities cited in note 9 of chapter 1, and also M. HARRIS & D. SPILLER, AFTER DECISION: IMPLEMENTATION OF JUDICIAL DECREES IN CORRECTIONAL SETTINGS (A.B.A. 1976); J. JACOBS, STATEVILLE: THE PENITENTIARY IN MASS SOCIETY (1977). On the structural decree more generally, *see* O. FISS, INJUNCTIONS 1, 415–81 (1972); Chayes, *The Role of the Judge in Public Law Litigation*, 89 HARV. L. REV. 1281 (1976).

5. 380 U.S. 145 (1965).

6. J. HIGH, A TREATISE ON THE LAW OF INJUNCTIONS 3 (1873).

7. Bell v. Southwell, 376 F.2d 659 (5th Cir. 1967).

8. Hills v. Gautreaux, 425 U.S. 284 (1976).

9. This individuated quality probably explains why the issuance of an injunction is thought to resemble the issuance of a command rather than the promulgation of a rule of conduct.

10. *See* Swann v. Charlotte-Mecklenburg Bd. of Educ., 402 U.S. 1, 6, 14–16, 31–32 (1971); United States v. Montgomery County Bd. of Educ., 395 U.S. 225, 227 (1969).

11. *See* Fiss, *Groups and the Equal Protection Clause,* 5 PHIL. & PUB. AFF. 107 (1976), reprinted in EQUALITY AND PREFERENTIAL TREATMENT (M. Cohen, T. Nagel, & T. Scanlon, eds. 1977).

12. *See* Potts v. Flax, 313 F.2d 284 (5th Cir. 1963). *See generally Developments in the Law—Class Actions,* 89 HARV. L. REV. 1318 (1976).

13. Fiss, *The Fate of An Idea Whose Time Has Come: Antidiscrimination Law in the Second Decade after* Brown v. Board of Education, 41 U. CHI. L. REV. 742, 753–54 (1974).

14. *Cf.* Golden State Bottling Co. v. NLRB, 414 U.S. 168 (1973) (NLRB may order successor company to reinstate employee when successor is bona fide purchaser with knowledge that predecessor committed unfair labor practice). *But see* Spomer v. Littleton, 414 U.S. 514 (1974) (remanding to consider mootness as a result of change of officeholder). *See generally* Comment, *Substitution under Federal Rule of Civil Procedure 25(d): Mootness and Related Problems,* 43 U. CHI. L. REV. 192 (1975).

15. Iveson v. Harris, 7 Ves. Jr. 251, 32 Eng. Rep. 102 (Ch. 1802). *Compare* Seaward v. Paterson [1897] 1 Ch. 545, 76 Law Times 215. On this topic generally, *see* Rendleman, *Beyond Contempt: Obligors to Injunctions,* 53 TEX. L. REV. 873 (1975).

16. Chase Nat'l Bank v. City of Norwalk, 291 U.S. 431, 437 (1934).

17. In Title I of the Civil Rights Act of 1968, Pub. L. No. 90–284, tit. I, 82 Stat. 73 (codified principally at 18 U.S.C. §§ 245, 2101, 2102 (1970)), the principle of this law is reaffirmed and the penalties stiffened.

18. Lee v. Macon County Bd. of Educ., 221 F. Supp. 297 (M.D. Ala. 1963), 222 F. Supp. 485 (M.D. Ala. 1963), 231 F. Supp. 743, 772 (M.D. Ala. 1964), 267 F. Supp. 458 (M.D. Ala. 1967), *aff'd sub nom.* Wallace v. United States, 389 U.S. 215 (1967) (per curiam); United States v. Barnett, 330 F.2d 369, 374–75 (5th Cir. 1963), *question certified answered in the negative,* 376 U.S. 681 (1964) (on facts of case contemnors have no right to trial by jury).

19. United States v. Hall, 472 F.2d 261, 267 (5th Cir. 1972). *See*

generally Comment, *Community Resistance to School Desegregation: Enjoining the Undefinable Class,* 44 U. CHI. L. REV. 111 (1976).

20. *See generally* D. DOBBS, HANDBOOK ON THE LAW OF REMEDIES 93–94 (1973); Dobbs, *Contempt of Court: A Survey,* 56 CORNELL L. REV. 183, 186–220 (1971).

21. *See* p. 27.

22. United States v. Trans-Missouri Freight Ass'n, 166 U.S. 290, 342–43 (1897). The only pre-*Debs* Sherman Act proceeding to reach the Supreme Court was United States v. E. C. Knight Co., 156 U.S. 1 (1895); that was an injunction proceeding, brought by the United States, but dismissed on other grounds.

23. In United States v. Brand Jewelers, Inc., 318 F. Supp. 1293, 1297 (S.D.N.Y. 1970), the court sustained the Attorney General's authority to sue to enjoin the practice of obtaining default judgments without proper service of notice. Other courts have permitted similar action by the Attorney General in allowing him to intervene in a suit challenging the constitutionality of a state's commitment and detainment statutes. *See* Alexander v. Hall, 64 F.R.D. 152 (D.S.C. 1974). In United States v. Solomon, 419 F. Supp. 358, 365–68 (D. Md. 1976), *aff'd*, 46 U.S.L.W. 2241 (4th Cir. Oct. 12, 1977), however, the court declined to follow *Brand Jewelers* in a case involving a mental institution; and in Estelle v. Justice, 426 U.S. 925 (1976), a prison case, three justices dissented from the denial of certiorari and revealed their unease with the practice of inviting the United States to participate as an amicus and allowing it to intervene without statutory authorization. The opinion dissenting from the denial of certiorari was written by Justice Rehnquist, and joined by Justices Burger and Powell. For the origins of this practice, *see* O. FISS, INJUNCTIONS 618–19 (1972).

24. Pub. L. No. 85–315, § 131, 71 Stat. 634 (current version at 42 U.S.C. § 1971(c) (1970)).

25. Pub. L. No. 86–449, § 101, 74 Stat. 86 (current version at 18 U.S.C. § 1509 (1970)).

26. Pub. L. No. 88–352, § 206, 78 Stat. 241 (codified at 42 U.S.C. § 2000a–5 (1970)).

27. Pub. L. No. 90–284, § 813, 82 Stat. 73 (codified at 42 U.S.C. § 3613 (1970)).

28. Equal Employment Opportunity Act of 1972, Pub. L. No. 92–

261, § 5, 86 Stat. 103 (amending 42 U.S.C. § 2000e–6(c) to (e) (1970)).

29. *See* the material referred to in note 13, chapter 2, plus the Boston school case (Morgan v. Hennigan, 379 F. Supp. 410 (D. Mass. 1974), *aff'd sub nom.* Morgan v. Kerrigan, 509 F.2d 580 (1st Cir. 1974), *cert. denied*, 421 U.S. 963 (1975); Morgan v. Kerrigan, 388 F. Supp. 581 (D. Mass. 1975); 401 F. Supp. 216 (D. Mass. 1975), *aff'd*, 530 F.2d 401 (1st Cir. 1976); 409 F. Supp. 1141 (D. Mass. 1975), *aff'd*, Morgan v. McDonough, 540 F.2d 527 (1st Cir. 1976)); the Coney Island school case (Hart v. Community School Bd. of Educ., 383 F. Supp. 699 (E.D.N.Y. 1974); 383 F. Supp. 769 (E.D.N.Y. 1974), *aff'd*, 512 F.2d 37 (2d Cir. 1975)); and Harris, *The Title VII Administrator: A Case Study in Judicial Flexibility*, 60 CORNELL L. REV. 53 (1974).

30. As reflected in cases such as Washington v. Davis, 426 U.S. 229 (1976), and Beer v. United States, 425 U.S. 130 (1976), the Burger Court has embarked on the strategy of treating the civil rights statutes as something more than a delegation, finding special significance in words used by the legislature in these statutes (so as to confine an effect theory to statutory claims, and leave a bad-purpose theory to govern constitutional claims). This seems at odds with the legislative history of these civil rights statutes. Congress saw itself either as extending the coverage of the Civil War amendments, thereby overcoming the state action limitation, or as devising new enforcement techniques. It did not view itself as annunciating the substantive standard; indeed, the so-called special words of the civil rights statutes—such as the word "effect"—were lifted by the legislative draftsmen (often attorneys in the Civil Rights Division) from judicial opinions construing the constitutional commands (*e.g.*, Judge Wisdom's opinion in United States v. Louisiana, 225 F. Supp. 353 (E.D. La. 1963), *aff'd*, 380 U.S. 145 (1965)); *see* Fiss, Gaston County v. United States: *Fruition of the Freezing Principle*, 1969 SUP. CT. REV. 379, 420–22.

31. 391 U.S. 194 (1968).

32. 422 U.S. 454, 475–79 (1975). For an earlier case with a different conclusion, rejecting the principle of progressivity, see United States v. R. L. Polk and Co., 438 F.2d 377 (6th Cir. 1971) (corporation entitled to jury trial where fine would exceed $500).

33. *See generally* Damaška, *Structures of Authority and Compara-*

tive Criminal Procedure, 84 YALE L.J. 480, 488–91, 513–15 (1975). Even the federal appellate system is decentralized, with the task of appellate review—the task of supervising the work of the trial courts—falling largely to the eleven courts of appeal, the work of the Supreme Court being more and more confined to the resolution of important questions of public law.

34. *See* Justice Rehnquist's concurring opinion in Albemarle Paper Co. v. Moody, 422 U.S. 405, 441 (1975), where he perceives the functional equivalence of trial judge discretion and the jury trial right, and argues, in the case of backpay, that if you do not have one, you must have the other.

35. Judge Johnson's practice of using three-judge courts regardless of whether they are required by statute might be viewed as a means of minimizing the personalization. *See* Lee v. Macon County Bd. of Educ., 267 F. Supp. 458 (M.D. Ala. 1967), *aff'd sub nom.* Wallace v. United States, 389 U.S. 215 (1967) (per curiam). More recently, the Supreme Court has expressed a dissatisfaction with this practice, *see* Costello v. Wainwright, 97 S. Ct. 1191 (1977) (per curiam); Morales v. Turman, 97 S. Ct. 1189 (1977) (per curiam). *See* Estelle v. Justice, referred to in note 23, this chapter, for an analogous reaction to another of Judge Johnson's practices.

36. There are parallels between the interlocutory process and certain pretrial procedures in the criminal system, such as the bail determination, and a comparison of the two might be illuminating.

37. *See* Section A of chapter 3 for the rules that may be imposed on the issuance of interlocutory injunctions to minimize their dangers.

38. 388 U.S. 307 (1967).

39. Certain structural features of the motion to vacate the temporary restraining order should preclude it from being deemed a sufficient opportunity for testing the constitutional validity of the order: (a) the motion is made to the same judge that issued the order; (b) the denial of the motion to vacate, like the grant of the temporary restraining order, is not appealable, and thus if issued by a state court, not reviewable by a federal tribunal; (c) the time constraints prevent the litigants from adequately preparing the facts and the law in support of the motion; and (d) since, by definition, the defendant against whom the restraining order has been issued is not yet participating in an ongoing

trial-sequence, and might still be without counsel, there is no basis for engaging the ordinary presumption that inaction, the failure to file a motion to vacate, should be construed as a strategic litigative choice, as a waiver of the opportunity to test the constitutional validity of the order.

40. *See* Frankel, *The Search for Truth: An Umpireal View*, 123 U. PA. L. REV. 1031 (1975); Damaška, *Presentation of Evidence and Factfinding Precision*, 123 U. PA. L. REV. 1083 (1975); Goldstein, *Reflections on Two Models: Inquisitorial Themes in American Criminal Procedure*, 26 STAN. L. REV. 1009 (1974).

41. *See* pp. 36–37.

42. *Cf.* Williams v. New York, 337 U.S. 241 (1949) (after fair trial defendant need not be confronted with witnesses whose testimony judge relies upon to impose sentence).

43. *See* Mayberry v. Pennsylvania, 400 U.S. 455, 463–66 (1971); Taylor v. Hayes, 418 U.S. 488 (1974); Codispoti v. Pennsylvania, 418 U.S. 506 (1974).

44. Here I have in mind a narrow conception of victim. One might begin to include the costs "to society" (*e.g.,* disutility caused by having something occur that a majority wishes not to occur), but that expansion blurs the distinction between liability rules and criminal prohibitions and does not strike me as analytically useful.

45. *See* pp. 74–80.

46. *See* the material referred to in note 20, this chapter.

47. To the extent that the criminal contempt sanction and the conditional order utilize imprisonment rather than a fine, they may bring about compliance with the norm through incapacitation, provided the rule of conduct is one that can be violated only if the defendant is physically free (as, for example, a rule against trespass). This overlap of deterrence and incapacitation is prevalent in the criminal regime, especially when the period of confinement reflects judgments about dangerousness.

48. Awkward though not inconceivable: with in-kind judgments the functional equivalent of seizure and sale would be some form of receivership, where a judicial officer would be put in charge of the defendant and would dispense the benefits according to the terms of the decree. *Cf.* two school desegregation receivership cases, Turner v.

Goolsby, 255 F. Supp. 724 (S.D. Ga. 1965) (Taliaferro County) and Morgan v. Kerrigan, 409 F. Supp. 1141 (D. Mass. 1975), *aff'd*, Morgan v. McDonough, 540 F.2d 527 (1st Cir. 1976) (Boston).

49. From this perspective, the structural injunction might profitably be compared to the parole and probation components of the criminal process.

III.   The Remedial Hierarchy

1. *See* O'Shea v. Littleton, 414 U.S. 488, 502–04 (1974).

2. 283 U.S. 697, 716 (1931). In our time that example has become the limiting case of the prior restraint doctrine's bar, conditioning the issuance of an injunction upon a showing "that publication must *inevitably, directly,* and *immediately* cause the occurrence of an event kindred to imperiling the safety of a transport already at sea." New York Times Co. v. United States, 403 U.S. 713, 726–27 (1971) (Brennan, J., concurring) (emphasis added). *See also* the concurring opinion of Stewart, J., joined by White, J., requiring harm to the nation that is "direct, immediate, and irreparable." *Id.* at 730. More recently, in Nebraska Press Ass'n v. Stuart, 427 U.S. 539 (1976), Chief Justice Burger paid homage to the prior restraint doctrine and the tradition of *Near v. Minnesota,* and yet judged the orders at issue by the discounted clear-and-present danger test of Dennis v. United States, 341 U.S. 494 (1951), a standard that is weaker than that used to judge subsequent restraints, either in the 1960s or 1970s. Justice Brennan wrote a separate concurrence in *Nebraska Press* in protest against this dilution of the prior restraint doctrine (or maybe even of the general First Amendment standard itself). He managed to obtain the votes of Stewart and Marshall and to provoke a sympathetic statement by Stevens. There is also a separate statement by White, and though that opinion is unclear, its very existence may well signal an uneasiness with the Chief Justice's treatment of the prior restraint doctrine and an intention to preserve the position he ambiguously took in *New York Times*, indicating that prior restraints are to be judged by the most stringent First Amendment standard. If so, the Chief Justice may not have been speaking for the Court in *Nebraska Press.*

3. For an account of the prosecution and the strike in general *see* A. LINDSEY, THE PULLMAN STRIKE (1942).

4. UNITED STATES STRIKE COMMISSION, REPORT ON THE CHICAGO STRIKE OF JUNE–JULY, 1894, S. EXEC. DOC. NO. 7, 53d Cong., 3rd Sess. XL (1895).

5. 320 Mass. 528, 70 N.E.2d 241 (1946).

6. *Id.* at 533–34, 70 N.E.2d at 244.

7. 319 U.S. 157 (1943).

8. 401 U.S. 37 (1971).

9. *See* note 1, chapter 3.

10. *See* Hazeltine, *The Early History of English Equity* in ESSAYS IN LEGAL HISTORY 261, 285 (P. Vinogradoff ed. 1913).

11. Pittsburgh Press Co. v. Pittsburgh Comm'n on Human Relations, 413 U.S. 376, 390 (1973) (emphasis added).

12. *See* Carroll v. President and Comm'rs of Princess Anne, 393 U.S. 175, 180–85 (1968).

13. American Cyanamid Co. v. Ethicon Ltd., [1975] A.C. 396 (H. L.). For cases discussing the implications of the *American Cyanamid* decision *see In re* Lord Cable [1977] W.L.R. 7, 19–20 (Ch. D.); Hubbard v. Pitt, [1976] Q.B. 142 (C.A.); Fellowes & Son v. Fisher, [1976] Q.B. 122 (C.A.); Bryanston Finance Ltd. v. De Vries (No. 2), [1976] Ch. 63 (C.A.).

14. *See* New York Times Co. v. United States, 403 U.S. 713 (1971). In another case, however, a federal district judge enjoined the publication of a book by a former CIA employee who had signed a secrecy agreement both before he was employed and upon resignation. United States v. Marchetti, 466 F.2d 1309 (4th Cir. 1972), *cert. denied*, 409 U.S. 1063 (1972).

15. Organization for a Better Austin v. Keefe, 402 U.S. 415 (1971). The injunction was called "temporary" by the issuing court but was treated by the Supreme Court as a final one, explicitly so. *Id.* at 418 n.*

16. *See In re* Herndon, 394 U.S. 399 (1969); Lee v. Macon County Bd. of Educ., 267 F. Supp. 458 (M.D. Ala. 1967), *aff'd sub nom.* Wallace v. United States, 389 U.S. 215 (1967) (per curiam). For a discussion of these cases and their implications for this issue, *see* O. FISS, INJUNCTIONS 645–90 (1972).

17. Build of Buffalo, Inc. v. Sedita, 441 F.2d 284, 287 (2d Cir. 1971).

18. *Compare In re* Murchison, 349 U.S. 133 (1955), with Codispoti v. Pennsylvania, 418 U.S. 506 (1974) (allowing summary trial of contemnor by same judge who is object of the contemptuous act "where the necessity of circumstances warrants").

19. On a more minor scale the jury argument is vulnerable for its lack of generality: at best it would justify subordinating the injunction to damage actions and criminal prosecutions, but not to remedies such as habeas corpus (*see* O'Shea v. Littleton, *supra* note 1, this chapter) or the criminal defense (*see* Younger v. Harris and Douglas v. City of Jeannette, *supra* notes 7 and 8, this chapter), for these remedies cannot be viewed as preservative of the right to trial by jury.

20. *See* Duncan v. Louisiana, 391 U.S. 145, 162 n.35 (1968).

21. If a conditional order utilized a fine, the jury could also decide the amount of the fine for each day of noncompliance.

22. I put to one side the possibility of utilizing the Seventh Amendment; it would probably be easier to say that conditional order civil contempt is a "crime" than a "suit at common law," and the Court would, in any event, have to deal with the special problems arising from the nonincorporation of that Amendment.

23. Williams v. Florida, 399 U.S. 78, 86–103 (1970); Colgrove v. Battin, 413 U.S. 149, 157–60 (1973).

24. Although federal criminal juries must be unanimous, the Supreme Court has held that state juries need not reach unanimous decisions; *see* Johnson v. Louisiana, 406 U.S. 356 (1972); Apodaca v. Oregon, 406 U.S. 404 (1972).

25. *See* D.E.C. Yale, *Introduction* to Lord Nottingham's "Manual of Chancery Practice" and "Prolegomena of Chancery and Equity" (1965); D.E.C. Yale, *Introduction* to Lord Nottingham's Chancery Cases ix (Selden Society vol. 73, 1957); Cook, *The Powers of Courts of Equity*, 15 Colum. L. Rev. 37, 106 (1915).

26. *See, e.g.,* Walker v. Sauvinet, 92 U.S. 90 (1876); Olesen v. Trust Co. of Chicago, 245 F.2d 522, 524 (7th Cir. 1957); Hurtado v. California, 110 U.S. 516 (1884) (grand juries). *See also* cases cited in notes 23 and 24 of this chapter.

27. *See* the discussion of the constitutional prohibition against Bills of Attainder in Nixon v. Administrator of General Services, 45 U.S.L.W.

4917, 4929–33 (Sup. Ct. June 28, 1977), limiting the proscription against legislative specificity in United States v. Brown, 381 U.S. 437 (1965). In *Nixon* the Court made clear that "specificity—the fact that it refers to appellant by name—does not automatically offend the Bill of Attainder Clause." 45 U.S.L.W. 4930. The question seemed to be whether the "appellant constituted a legitimate class of one," whether "the focus of the enactment can be fairly and rationally understood." *Id.* "Moreover," the Court also made clear, "even if the specificity element were deemed to be satisfied here, the Bill of Attainder Clause would not automatically be implicated." *Id.* "[O]ne who complains of being attainted must establish that the legislature's action constituted punishment and not merely the legitimate regulation of conduct." 45 U.S.L.W. 4931 n.40.

28. *See generally* H. PITKIN, THE CONCEPT OF REPRESENTATION (1967).

29. Why must we have this mechanism of accountability? Presumably if the method of choosing the jury were sufficient to assure a representative group (in the pictorial sense) on every conceivable issue, then an accountability mechanism would be superfluous. The jury could both stand for and speak for the public. But given the gap between the size of the panel (*e.g.*, one hundred) and the size of the universe to be represented (*e.g.*, one million), the distortions to be introduced (by both preemptory and cause challenges) in reducing the panel down to twelve or six, and the fact that the selection must precede full public discussion of the issue, it is hard to imagine such a perfect selection mechanism. That is why we have public policy formulated by legislatures, who debate in public and must stand for reelection, rather than by randomly selected juries.

30. For a discussion of the value of the jury as an aresponsible agency, *see* G. CALABRESI & P. BOBBITT, TRAGIC CHOICES (1978).

31. A variant of this argument, viewing an administrative agency as exercising power delegated to it by a legislature, and as more susceptible to popular pressures than a court, might suggest a subordination of the injunction to administrative remedies. This argument has a special saliency with structural decrees, where it is coupled with the myth of the expertise of administrative agencies. I for one do not believe that

the administrative agency has any expert knowledge that cannot be conveyed to and evaluated by a court; the rest of the argument collapses for the reasons set forth in this section.

32. *See* pp. 24–25.

33. United States v. Carolene Prods. Co., 304 U.S. 144, 152 n.4 (1938).

34. 319 U.S. 105 (1943).

35. 319 U.S. 157 (1943).

36. 97 S. Ct. 1428 (1977). I discuss this case, the other *Douglas* progeny, and the general issues raised in this section in *Dombrowski,* 86 YALE L.J. 1103 (1977).

37. To support such an irrebuttable presumption, Justice Rehnquist can do no more than quote from Article VI of the Constitution, proclaiming that state judges are bound to uphold the Constitution. Huffman v. Pursue, Ltd., 420 U.S. 592, 611 (1975).

38. *See, e.g.,* the statements by Chancellor Kent in Jerome v. Ross, 7 Johns. Ch. 315, 333 (N.Y. 1823).

39. If the purpose is to establish a new norm of conduct, and if there is no fear that the defendant will violate that norm in the future, then no restraint is necessary. A declaratory judgment could be substituted for the injunction, for it is simply an injunction without sanctions. The distinction is explored on pp. 51–74 of my casebook INJUNCTIONS (1972) and also on pp. 1122–23, 1144–48 of the article referred to in note 36 of this chapter.

40. The overbreadth doctrine modifies traditional notions of standing (relieving the plaintiff of showing that his conduct is protected) and enlarges the scope of the judgment (invalidating the statute in all its applications), but does not introduce a new substantive standard as to what speech can be reached by the state.

41. Kalven, *The Supreme Court, 1970 Term—Foreword: Even When a Nation Is at War,* 85 HARV. L. REV. 3, 34 (1971).

42. When the general counsel of the *New York Times* spoke at the University of Chicago Law School on November 5, 1971, he said the commitment to abide by the injunction was a mistake and ill-conceived.

43. In affidavits filed in a later case, the newspapers involved in the *Pentagon Papers Case* said they would "not feel bound to observe such

an injunction [ordering them not to publish] under different circumstances in the future." N.Y. Times, Jan. 21, 1973, § 1, at 26, col. 3. The case in which they filed the affidavits was United States v. Dickinson, 465 F.2d 496 (5th Cir. 1972), *after remand*, 476 F.2d 373 (5th Cir.), *cert. denied*, 414 U.S. 979 (1973).

44. *See* p. 28.

45. *See* N.Y. Times, June 15, 1971, at 1, col. 8.

46. I put to one side the risk of interdependence—that the criminal contempt may make a criminal prosecution more likely. For it seems just as likely that the criminal contempt might work in the opposite direction, that is, to reduce the certainty of a criminal prosecution— one punishment is enough. Nor do I think an argument on behalf of the prior restraint doctrine can be constructed out of the cumulative impact of the injunction, either in terms of compounding the sanction of the criminal statute or facilitating the criminal prosecution. That would be a point about cumulation, not the injunction, and might be as true of the damage action or the declaratory judgment as the injunction.

47. The damage award might include punitive damages and of course be of staggering proportions. Consider the $500,000 award at stake in New York Times Co. v. Sullivan, 376 U.S. 255 (1964), or the $1.25 million award in the recent Mississippi NAACP boycott case, *see* N.Y. Times, Aug. 12, 1976, at 39, col. 1.

48. The Supreme Court in its *Debs* opinion mischaracterizes that testimony by Eugene Debs and suggests that what ended the strike was the injunction—all a strategem to legitimate the labor injunction. *See In re* Debs, 158 U.S. 564, 597–98 (1895). For Debs's testimony before the Strike Commission, see UNITED STATES STRIKE COMMISSION, *supra* note 4, this chapter, at 142–44.

49. *See e.g.*, Becker, *Crime and Punishment: An Economic Approach*, 76 J. POLITICAL ECON. 169 (1968).

50. *See* O. W. HOLMES, *The Path of the Law* in COLLECTED LEGAL PAPERS 167 (1921).

51. *See* pp. 55–56, this chapter.

52. *See* H.L.A. HART, THE CONCEPT OF LAW (1961).

53. *See generally* Calabresi & Melamed, *Property Rules, Liability Rules, and Inalienability: One View of the Cathedral*, 85 HARV. L. REV.

1089 (1972). *See also* Block & Lind, *Crime and Punishment Reconsidered,* 4 J. LEGAL STUD. 241 (1975).

54. *See* R. NOZICK, ANARCHY, STATE, AND UTOPIA 65–71 (1974). Nozick also seems to be concerned with the fear of those who are never in fact victimized, for they will never receive compensation (for their fear). But the nonvictims do not seem to pose any special problems; all are assured that if they become victims they will be fully compensated.

55. *See* O. FISS, INJUNCTIONS 91 (1972); Note, *Injunction Negotiations: An Economic, Moral, and Legal Analysis,* 27 STAN. L. REV. 1563 (1975); the Calabresi and Melamed article referred to in note 53, this chapter; and Michelman, *Pollution as a Tort: A Non-Accidental Perspective on Calabresi's Costs,* 80 YALE L.J. 647 (1971).

56. This appears to have been the situation in Jerome v. Ross, 7 Johns. Ch. 315 (N.Y. 1823), one of the classic American precedents for the irreparable injury requirement.

57. United States v. W. T. Grant Co., 345 U.S. 629, 633 (1953). *Cf.* Hecht Co. v. Bowles, 321 U.S. 321, 328–31 (1944).

58. Striking examples of the kinds of judgments that have to be made in noninjunctive contexts are found in the 1976 death penalty cases, Woodson v. North Carolina, 428 U.S. 280 (1976); Jurek v. Texas, 428 U.S. 262 (1976); Proffitt v. Florida, 428 U.S. 242 (1976); Gregg v. Georgia, 428 U.S. 153 (1976).

59. As I noted in chapter 2, such hints could be found in the emphasis given to the defendants' failure to file a motion to dissolve before disobeying, and that the injunction involved was not patently invalid. Note could also be taken of the fact that *Walker* permitted the states to adopt a contrary rule; it did not require such a rule, and, of course, the Supreme Court might adopt a different rule for the federal courts.

60. Brandenburg v. Ohio, 395 U.S. 444 (1969). For the evolution of the different legacies, see Gunther, *Learned Hand and the Origins of Modern First Amendment Doctrine: Some Fragments of History,* 27 STAN. L. REV. 719 (1975); and the soon-to-be-published manuscript of Harry Kalven, A WORTHY TRADITION.

61. *See* Dennis v. United States, 341 U.S. 494, 579 (1951) (Black, J., dissenting); *see generally* Nathanson, *Freedom of Association and the Quest for Internal Security: Conspiracy from Dennis to Dr. Spock,* 65 NW. L. REV. 153 (1970).

IV.   The Legacy: New Perspectives on the Relationship
between Rights and Remedies

1. 386 U.S. 547 (1967).
2. 415 U.S. 651 (1974).
3. Bivens v. Six Unknown Named Agents of Fed. Bureau of Narcotics, 403 U.S. 388 (1971); Wood v. Strickland, 420 U.S. 308 (1975).
4. This should not be surprising since it is in large part defined by the enterprise.
5. Clark, Book Review, 45 U. COLO. L. REV. 163, 168 (1973).
6. *See* pp. 36–37.
7. There is a special irony to this charge. Conceived in the boldest terms, the ambition of the administrative law system might have been to restructure industries put under its jurisdiction, but the truth of the matter is that that ambition has not been realized. The administrative law system, so anxious about its own legitimacy, in fact became judicialized, content to issue cease-and-desist orders (the counterpart of the preventive injunctions), and to avoid structural reform. In recent years the task of structural reformation of public institutions (schools, prisons, and mental hospitals) has been taken up by the courts, and it remains to be seen whether this judicial experience—by example and by lending legitimacy to coercive structural reformation—will revitalize the administrative system, encourage it to attempt a realization of its boldest ambitions.
8. 423 U.S. 362 (1976). I discussed this case and *Littleton* and the Burger Court's attitude toward structural injunctions in *Dombrowski*, 86 YALE L.J. 1103, 1148–60 (1977).
9. *See* the article by Damaška, referred to in note 39 of chapter 2, criticizing Thibaut, Walker, & Lind, *Adversary Presentation and Bias in Legal Decisionmaking*, 86 HARV. L. REV. 386 (1972).
10. These themes are explored in the article referred to in note 11 of chapter 2.

Indices

SUBJECT INDEX

Administrative agencies: role in structural reform, 106n*31*, 110n7

Adversarial model of litigation, 30; norm of impartiality, 50; questioning importance, 93. *See also* Judicial role; Structural injunction

Amicus curiae, 31, 92, 99n*23*. *See also* Attorney General; Structural injunction

Antiobstruction injunction, 17. *See also* Interlocutory injunction

Anti-Progressivism injunction, 2–3, 4, 7, 9, 23, 60; decisional authority, 25, 89; no statutory authority, 59

Antitrust, 59; divestiture cases, 10; authority of Attorney General, 20–21. *See also* Clayton Act; Sherman Act

Attorney General, 71, 72; policing performance, 22, 31, 92; *amicus curiae*, 92, 99n*23*; intervention, 99n*23*
—bringing suit: without statutory authorization, 99n*23*; with statutory authorization, 20–22, 88–89. *See also* Department of Justice; Special masters; Structural injunction

Barnett, Governor Ross, 17

Berger, Raoul (*Government by Judiciary*), 5

Bills of Attainder, 105n*27*

Black, Justice Hugo, 10

Boudin, Louis (*Government by Judiciary*), 5

Brandeis, Justice Louis, 16

Brennan, Justice William, 103n*2*

Brewer, Justice David, 96n*3*

Bureaucracy, judge-created, 23, 93. *See also* Judicial role; Structural injunction

Burger, Chief Justice Warren, 99n*23*, 103n2

Chancery, 42–43, 44–45, 68; absence of jury trial right, 50–51

Civil disobedience, 70–71, 72–73, 74. *See also* Obedience to judicial decrees; Prior restraint doctrine

Civil rights injunction, 9; individuation, 13, 14, 15; antiobstruction, 17; legislative authorization, 21, 59–60; decisional authority, 23–25; undermining hierarchy of remedies, 43–44, 87–90; equal protection claim, 60. *See also* Reparative injunction; Structural injunction

Civil rights statutes, 100n*30*
—Civil Rights Act of 1957 (42 U.S.C. § 1971 (c) (1970)), 21
—Civil Rights Act of 1960 (18 U.S.C. § 1509 (1970)), 21
—Civil Rights Act of 1964 (42 U.S.C. § 2000a-5 (1970)), 21, 25
—Civil Rights Act of 1968 (18 U.S.C. §§ 245, 2101, 2102 (1970); 42 U.S.C. § 3613 (1970)), 21, 25
—Equal Opportunity Employment Act of 1972 (amending 42 U.S.C. § 2000e-6 (c) to (e) (1970)), 22
—42 U.S.C. § 1983 (1970), 66

Clark, Homer, 92

Class actions, 15. *See also* Groups

Clayton Act (15 U.S.C. § 25 (1970); 18 U.S.C. § 3691 (1970); 29 U.S.C. § 52 (1970); F.R.C.P. 65), 3, 15, 16, 47

Comity: alternative to irreparable injury requirement, 68

Compensation, 74–80, 90; in-kind (re-

Case Index